DISEASES

2nd Revised Edition

Volume 3

Crossed eyes to Fetus

Bryan Bunch

EDITOR
SCIENTIFIC PUBLISHING

GROLIER
EDUCATIONAL

Editor: Bryan Bunch

Design and production: G & H SOHO, Inc.
Design: Gerry Burstein
Prepress: Kathie Kounouklos

Writers:

Barbara Branca
Bryan Bunch
Barbara A. Darga
Betsy Feist
Gene R. Hawes
Wendy B. Murphy
Karin L. Rhines
Jenny Tesar
Bruce Wetterau
Gray Williams

Editorial assistant:
Marianne Bunch

Copyediting and index:
Felice Levy

Creative assistance:
Pam Forde

Illustrators:

Photographs:
Karin L. Rhines

Icons:
Steve Virkus and Karen Presser

Medical Illustrations:
Jean Cassels
Leslie Dunlap
Pamela Johnson
Joel Snyder

Library of Congress Cataloging in Publication Data

Main entry under title:
Diseases
v. < >' cm
Includes bibliographical references and index.
Summary: Alphabetically arranged articles present medical information
on more than 500 diseases, discussing causes, symptoms, stages of the
disease, its likelihood of striking, treatments, prevention, and long-term effects.

Set ISBN: 0-7172-5688-X

1. Diseases—Encyclopedias, Juvenile. [1. Diseases—
Encyclopedias.] I. Grolier Educational Corporation
R130.5 D57 1996
616.003—dc20   96-27606
                                          CIP
                                          AC

Revised edition published 2003.
First published in the United States in 1997 by
Grolier Educational, Sherman Turnpike, Danbury, CT 06816

Crossed eyes

By the age of six months most babies can focus both eyes on the same object at the same time. When the two eyes point in different directions, the condition is called crossed eyes if the direction of vision is inward or *walleye* if the direction is outward. The medical name for either misalignment of vision is *strabismus* (struh-BIHZ-muhs). The expression "wall-eye" is seldom used anymore; in this entry the more common modern usage of "crossed eyes" indicates either form of strabismus.

Cause: Most people with crossed eyes are born with the condition (it is *congenital),* which is caused by a defect in one of the nerves that control the eye muscles. The condition is more common in children with cerebral palsy or hydrocephalus. Crossed eyes may develop in older people as a result of injury, cataracts, diabetes, stroke, or other illness.

Noticeable symptoms: In crossed eyes one or both of the eyes turns up, down, in, or out. A person with crossed eyes may have double vision, particularly if he or she develops crossed eyes after having normal vision.

Diagnosis: A doctor will ask the patient to look at a pencil and alternately cover and uncover an eye. Movement of the eye as it is uncovered indicates a deviation. With a baby the doctor may do the penlight test: If the baby has crossed eyes, the light may be reflected from the pupil of one eye and from the iris of the other.

Treatment options: To strengthen and improve vision, a child with crossed eyes may wear an eye patch over the stronger eye, forcing the brain to rely on the weaker eye. A doctor also may prescribe exercises to strengthen the eye muscles. Special eyedrops and corrective glasses may be prescribed later. Sometimes surgery on the eye muscles is employed if other corrective measures fail. A recent technique is to inject a drug that relaxes the target muscle for several weeks; when the drug wears off, the eye muscle often functions normally.

Stages and progress: Among children born with crossed eyes, the brain usually accepts images from the stronger eye only; the image from the weaker eye is ignored. It is important to identify and correct crossed eyes as soon as possible. Otherwise the sight in the weaker eye may be lost. Infants should have eye examinations by the age of six months. The problem should not be ignored on the assumption that it will be outgrown.

Croup

DISEASE

TYPE: INFECTIOUS (VIRAL OR
        BACTERIAL)

See also
Coughs
Hemophilus influenzae **type B**
Infants and disease
Influenza
Laryngitis
Larynx
Respiratory system
Viruses and disease

At night parents hear their infant breathing noisily and rapidly. The child begins coughing with a sound similar to that of a barking seal. They suspect that their child has croup.

Cause: Croup, or acute *laryngotracheitis* (luh-RING-goh-TRAY-kee-IY-tuhs), is the general name for any infectious disease that has a particular barklike cough as its characteristic symptom. Such diseases are usually caused by one of several viruses, including the influenza A and B viruses. Sometimes croup is caused by a bacterial infection. The reason for the characteristic cough is that infection has attacked the voice box (larynx), causing the vocal cords to swell. But croup is a more generalized disease than laryngitis, in which a mild inflammation usually affects the larynx only.

Incidence: Croup is the most common illness in infants and children from three months to five years of age that leads to a visit to the pediatrician. Nearly all cases occur between one and three years of age. The younger the child, the greater the likelihood of severe symptoms.

Noticeable symptoms: Symptoms include fever, hoarseness, irritability, and a characteristic barking cough. Breathing may be noisy, and the child may gasp or choke on excess mucus in the throat. In more severe cases the child's chest sinks in deeply with each breath, drooling occurs, and the lips turn blue. *If breathing becomes difficult, consult a physician immediately;*

Phone doctor

Emergency Room

inflammation of the epiglottis may be involved, a possibly fatal condition.

Diagnosis: The pediatrician will examine the upper respiratory tract visually and listen to the sound of breathing with a stethoscope. If there is some doubt about the diagnosis, x-rays of the trachea can be helpful in determining the severity of the disease.

Treatment options: For mild cases children can be treated at home as long as they get bed rest and high humidity. Cool-mist humidifiers are recommended over steam vaporizers to loosen fluids and make breathing easier. Even taking a baby out into cooler air or into a bathroom with a running shower to increase humidity can help.

Children should be given liquids at room temperature to prevent dehydration, but no solid food. If a child has severe symptoms such as high fever, blue color, and distressed breathing, treatment at the emergency room is indicated. There the child may be given oxygen to breathe within a humid environment. A nebulizer may be used to break the croup with epinephrine, but no other medicines are used. Antibiotics are useless in viral infections, and cough medicines, especially those that contain opiates such as codeine, are harmful with croup.

Stages and progress: Symptoms may last for as little as one hour or worsen and then improve over several days. Symptoms generally occur more often at night—in the spasmodic form symptoms occur only at night and last a short time each night. In most cases the disease lasts from three to seven days. Sometimes the infection spreads to other parts of the respiratory system, causing pneumonia, ear infections, or infections of the airways of the lungs.

Prevention: Teaching even young children good health habits such as covering a sneeze or cough, not sharing eating utensils, and washing hands often can prevent the spread of respiratory infections. Also, if a child is recuperating from a cold, avoid exposure to cold air, which may trigger the disease.

| Cryptococcosis | *See* **Fungus diseases** |

Cryptosporidiosis

(KRIHP-toh-spuh-rihd-ee-OH-suhs)

DISEASE

TYPE: INFESTATION
(PARASITIC)

See also
Cramp
Diarrhea
Parasites and disease

During a six-week outbreak in 1993 in the Milwaukee area about 400,000 people experienced diarrhea and cramping. Thousands had to be hospitalized, and 100 died. The likely cause was identified as cryptosporidiosis.

Cause: A tiny parasite called *Cryptosporidium* causes cryptosporidiosis. The infection occurs when a person swallows water containing microscopic thick-walled reproductive structures of the parasite called *oocysts* (OH-uh-sihsts). Inside the body the oocyst enters the cells lining the intestinal tract. Here it reproduces and prevents the intestine from absorbing needed food and water.

Cryptosporidiosis is called a waterborne infection because it is transmitted from person to person through water rather than air or casual physical contact. But it can also be transmitted by direct contact with feces from an infected person or even a pet.

Incidence: When an outbreak such as that in Milwaukee occurs, it usually means that there has been a breakdown in a filtration plant. Since the Milwaukee outbreak public health officials throughout the United States have developed new guidelines to protect the public from future outbreaks of waterborne infections.

Noticeable symptoms: The major symptoms of cryptosporidiosis are episodes of frequent, watery diarrhea accompanied by severe abdominal cramps. Some people also experience fatigue, fever, nausea, and vomiting. The symptoms usually last about two weeks in people with healthy immune systems. Some infected people have no symptoms at all.

Diagnosis: If a doctor suspects cryptosporidiosis, he or she will do a fecal smear on a stool sample. Presence of oocysts will confirm the diagnosis.

Treatment options: The infection runs its course without medication in most instances. Some individuals, however, may lose so much water that they become dehydrated and require rehydration. Researchers are looking for medicines that will help people with immune system problems get rid of the infection.

Stages and progress: People who are already ill or under great stress when they become infected with *Cryptosporidium* may take longer to get well. When the first illness is over or the stress is reduced, the body can then successfully fight the cryptosporidiosis. In a person with a healthy immune response cryptosporidiosis is usually self-limiting.

However, unless overcome by a person's immune system, the microbe will continue to reproduce. People with serious immune system problems—such as those with AIDS—are more easily infected and have greater difficulty in fighting the parasite. Once *Cryptosporidium* is in the body, individuals with AIDS may never be able to get rid of it. Those with suppressed immune systems after organ transplant or during cancer treatment are also at risk.

Prevention: When *Cryptosporidium* reproduces in the body, some of the new oocysts that result are released in the feces. These oocysts can infect other individuals through water, anal-oral sex, or poor hygiene. Some public health experts believe that most cases of cryptosporidiosis that occur when the water supply is safe are the result of person-to-person transmission. People who care for individuals with cryptosporidiosis, especially individuals who are bedridden and using diapers, are at risk when changing the diapers and bathing the patient. In day care centers for children cryptosporidiosis can easily be transmitted person to person. Frequent, thorough hand washing is the best prevention.

Wash hands

When there is a waterborne outbreak of cryptosporidiosis, public health officials issue a "boil water alert." A notice is released that all water to be used for drinking, brushing teeth, and food must be boiled for one minute to destroy the oocysts. People with AIDS and other serious immune system problems may be advised to boil water they use for any purpose, including washing.

Boil water

Animals, including cats and dogs, can also have cryptosporidiosis. They can pass the infection to humans, and humans can pass the infection to them. Thorough hand washing after using the toilet and after playing with animals with diarrhea prevents humans from infecting their pets or being infected by them.

Cystic fibrosis
(SIHS-tihk fiy-BROH-sihs)

DISEASE

TYPE: GENETIC

See also
Exocrine glands
Genetic diseases
Lungs
Pancreas

Cystic fibrosis is a severe hereditary disease, first recognized in 1938, that affects the function of the exocrine glands. Some of these glands generate and release body fluids such as sweat and mucus. The disease causes these secretions to have low water content so that mucus becomes abnormally thick and sticky, and sweat is unusually salty.

In many people who have the disease the abnormal mucus blocks the ducts leading from the pancreas so that its digestive enzymes cannot reach the intestine. Affected individuals are likely to have a ravenous appetite yet remain malnourished and underweight no matter how much they eat. In time the insulin-producing cells of the pancreas may become damaged, causing diabetes.

Even more serious are the effects on the lungs and the *bronchial* (BRONG-kee-uhl) *passages* leading to them. Normally these are lined with a thin film of mucus, which protects them from germs and impurities in the air. The mucus is constantly regenerated, and hairlike cell projections called *cilia* (SIHL-ee-uh) sweep the mucus up the bronchial passages to the throat, where it can be swallowed and digested. But when the mucus is thick and sticky, it overwhelms the efforts of the cilia to remove it. Instead, it clogs the bronchial passages and hinders the absorption of oxygen from the lungs. Breathing is difficult, and the body is chronically starved for oxygen. The stagnant mucus also harbors germs, so infections such as pneumonia are frequent and severe. Repeated infection and inflammation damage the lungs, leading to the respiratory failure that is the most common cause of death from the disease.

Now that most people with cystic fibrosis live to be adults, it is at least theoretically possible for them to have children. But almost all affected men and a higher than usual percentage of women are infertile. All the children of an affected woman will be carriers for the disease and run a statistically higher risk of being affected themselves.

Cause: The disease can be caused by any of a large number of abnormal mutations in a single gene on chromosome number seven. The mutant gene is recessive—it must be inherited from both parents to have a harmful effect. Genetic testing can identify many (but not all) carriers of the defect.

Damage from cystic fibrosis

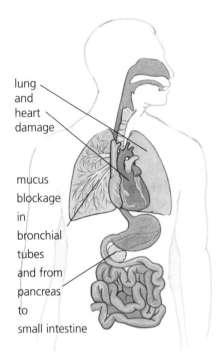

lung
and
heart
damage

mucus
blockage
in
bronchial
tubes
and from
pancreas
to
small intestine

Although the fundamental cause of cystic fibrosis is an ineffective gene for a single protein, the damage spreads throughout the body. Cells cannot release water, so the liquid around them thickens. This thick material clogs airways and other passages. Lungs cannot take in enough air. The heart works harder to move oxygen-poor blood. The digestive system also begins to fail. Furthermore, the weakened body is exposed to high levels of bacteria that thrive in the thick fluids.

A gene functions by causing the production of a specific protein. The protein in this case regulates the passage of compounds of chlorine—chlorides—out of cells. This in turn affects the passage of sodium and water molecules in and out of the cells. When the protein is absent or nonfunctional, the mucus produced in such organs as the lungs does not contain enough water and so becomes thick and sticky. The mucus becomes even thicker as the result of inflammation, which results in the accumulation of dead white blood cells in the inflamed tissues.

Because so many different mutations can cause cystic fibrosis, the disease is widely variable in its severity. Not all of those affected, for example, suffer blockage of the pancreatic ducts.

Incidence: Cystic fibrosis is a relatively common genetic disease. In the United States about 1,000 babies are born with it each year. About 30,000 American children and adults are affected, concentrated among Caucasians of northern European origin. About 1 in 28 Caucasian Americans is believed to be a carrier of the defective gene that causes the disease.

Noticeable symptoms: The disease usually shows up in infancy or childhood. Typical symptoms are breathlessness, wheezing, persistent coughing, and frequent respiratory infections. The affected person may also be constantly hungry yet underweight. Stools may be large and unusually smelly if the pancreas is involved.

Diagnosis: The simplest and most common method of diagnosing cystic fibrosis is a *sweat test;* this reveals an unusually high level of salt in the perspiration of an affected individual. This may be followed with chest x-rays, analysis of stools for pancreatic enzymes, and genetic testing.

Treatment options: At present the disease cannot be cured, but treatment has helped considerably to control its symptoms and harmful effects. Blocked pancreatic enzymes can be replaced, and vitamins and other dietary supplements help prevent malnutrition. Antibiotics are used to control pneumonia and other infections.

Much treatment centers on clearing mucus physically from the lungs and bronchial passages. For many years the main method has been to clap the chest and back to dislodge the mucus so it can be coughed up. This is sometimes supplemented by *postural drainage*—having the patient assume various positions (including upside down) that encourage the mucus to drain up and out of the lobes of the lungs.

In recent years an instrument called a flutter has also been used to loosen mucus. It looks like a smoking pipe; but when a patient blows into it, it sets up a rapid oscillation, or flutter, of varying air pressures in the breathing passages, shaking the mucus loose. Apparently even more effective is a machine-inflated vest that exerts varying pressures on the chest with the same result.

In cases of serious lung damage a lung transplant can prolong life.

Outlook: The best long-term prospect for cure lies in some form of *gene therapy,* which would enable the defective gene to be partly or completely replaced by a normal one. There have been a number of promising experiments but no completely satisfactory solution.

Cysts

DISEASE

TYPE: VARIOUS

An abnormal growth consisting of a closed sac filled with fluid or solid material is called a cyst. The material within the cyst is produced by the cells that make up the lining, or wall, of the cyst. Some cysts form during development of the embryo, but the majority form later in life.

Cause: Cysts form for a variety of reasons, depending to some degree on the tissue involved. Hormones are believed to play a role in the formation of cysts of the breast. Some cysts that form in the adrenal glands are caused by bacterial infections or by parasites. Baker's cysts, which form behind the knee inside the bend, may be associated with arthritis. The cause of other cysts is unknown.

Incidence: Many people develop cysts. For example, about 50% of premenopausal women experience cysts in the breast. Other common sites of cyst formation include the skin, ovaries, and kidneys. Liver cysts, cysts in glands, and cysts in ears are all possible.

Noticeable symptoms: If swelling near the surface of the body occurs, you may see or feel a lump. Otherwise you may experience some pain or discomfort. Since these symptoms may signal a variety of medical problems, it is wise to see a doctor.

Diagnosis: The actions taken by a doctor will depend on the location of the symptoms. For example, if pain and swelling occur along one of the long bones of the arm or leg, x-rays will be taken to determine if a bone cyst has formed. If the lump is in a breast, the doctor may *biopsy* some tissue—remove it for microscopic examination—to make certain that the lump is not cancerous.

Treatment options: Some cysts, such as Baker's cysts, do not usually require any treatment; they gradually heal and disappear. Other cysts, especially larger ones, may need to be drained. This is a simple procedure usually performed in a physician's office. A small incision is made in the cyst, the fluid is allowed to drain, and the area is covered with a bandage. In some cases the entire cyst must be surgically removed; for example, skin cysts may recur if the walls are not completely removed.

Dacryocystitis
(DAAK-ree-oh-sihs-TIY-tihs)

DISEASE

TYPE: MECHANICAL

It affects both the very young and people over 40. It can start suddenly and painfully or build up gradually over weeks or months. Dacryocystitis is inflammation of the tear sac, a pouch in the corner of the eye that collects tears.

Cause: Dacryocystitis occurs when the tubes, or ducts, from the tear sacs to the eye and nose become blocked and fluid is trapped. Bacteria reproduce in the trapped fluid and cause infection. Usually only one eye is affected.

Noticeable symptoms: The corner of the eye by the nose becomes red and may be painful and swollen. The eye may be watery and there may be pus in the corner when the area is pressed gently.

Diagnosis: A doctor can take a sample of the discharge to identify the bacteria that cause the infection. The doctor may also use dye or take x-rays to find the blockage.

Treatment: Dacryocystitis in babies often results because the ducts that carry tears away from the tear sacs are not fully developed, or the ducts may not have openings to the eyes and nose. Gently massaging the affected area several times a day can help to clear the blockage. As the baby grows the duct may open naturally. Antibiotics may be given to fight the infection. In some cases the duct is opened with minor surgery. Most babies with dacryocystitis outgrow the condition by their first birthday.

In adults dacryocystitis can result from a broken nose or other trauma to the face, an infection of the nose, or even thickening of the bones of the face that press against the ducts, making them narrower. If the condition is mild, warm compresses can be applied to the eye to relieve pain and discomfort and help the tear sacs drain. Antibiotics are prescribed if pus is present. A doctor will prescribe different antibiotics depending on which bacteria are present. If this does not clear the blockage, the doctor may insert a tiny tube into the tear duct and flush it with saline solution. If none of these treatments is successful, surgery to drain or even remove the tear sac can be performed. Usually, however, the less drastic treatments work.

Deafness

SYMPTOM

Many people have partial or complete loss of hearing, a condition known as deafness. Hearing loss may have existed since birth (*congenital deafness*), may be due to disease, or may occur as a result of aging.

Deafness that is congenital or that begins in early infancy may interfere with ability to learn spoken language. Deafness that comes later in life does not usually result in poor speech, but may induce the deaf person to become isolated, affecting mental health.

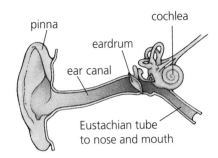

The outer ear, or pinna, focuses sound waves on the eardrum, which changes differences in air pressure into movement of bones. This movement shakes a liquid, which causes fine hairs to vibrate, a vibration that is felt by nerves and transmitted to the brain. Hearing, then, is a complex process that can go wrong at various places along the way.

Incidence: More than 28 million Americans have some form of hearing loss, including deafness. The number is heavily weighted toward older Americans, with 30 to 35% of those between 65 and 75 developing age-related hearing loss, a percentage that rises to 40% of those over 75. Many older people develop a form of hearing loss that cannot be prevented. Sounds become muffled, causing the listener to ask people to speak louder. The hearing-impaired may speak in a monotone or cup the ear to hear better. Some age-related hearing loss involves a loss of the high-pitched tones and a lack of ability to distinguish certain words.

Related symptoms: Conditions related to hearing loss include ringing in the ears, or tinnitus, as well as dizziness, or *vertigo*. The latter is usually caused by an infection of the inner ear, which is the location of the semicircular canals, the organs of balance. Problems of balance may or may not be associated with hearing loss.

The ear: The ear is usually described in terms of three main regions—the outer, middle, and inner.

■ The part of the ear that can be seen, known as the *pinna* (PIHN-nuh) or the *auricle* (AWR-ih-kuhl), funnels sound to the working parts of the ear, all of which are inside the skull. The pinna is connected by a passage called the ear canal to a membrane called the eardrum. The eardrum is the outermost part of the ear; it accomplishes any task other than the collection of sound waves. Even though the eardrum is hidden, the pinna, ear canal, and eardrum together make up the *outer ear.*

■ Sound is produced by changes in air pressure that move the eardrum rapidly back and forth. The *middle ear* contains three small bones that conduct the movements of the eardrum to the inner ear.

■ Finally, the *inner ear* contains the *cochlea* (KOK-lee-uh), a delicate organ of hearing in which actual sensory cells are found. The cochlea produces signals in the auditory nerve that the brain recognizes as specific sounds. The inner ear also contains organs of balance that are not involved in hearing.

Hearing loss caused by mechanical problems: Defects in some part of the ear are the most common cause of deafness.

In *conductive hearing loss* injury or abnormal growth in the outer or middle ear prevents sound from reaching the inner ear properly. Conductive hearing loss caused by blockage of the eustachian (yoo-STAY-shuhn) tube (which connects the ear to the nose and throat) leads to a kind of barrier called a *cholesteatoma* (koh-LEHS-tee-uh-TOH-muh), a lump of cells shed by the eardrum that blocks or partly blocks hearing.

A *punctured eardrum* may result when something sharp enters the ear canal and accidentally penetrates the delicate membrane. It can also occur when there is a sudden pressure buildup caused by an explosion or a deep dive into water. Such a puncture causes severe pain, bleeding from the ear, and hearing loss, which may or may not be permanent.

Sensorineural hearing loss involves damage to the inner ear or auditory nerve. Sensory hearing loss usually affects the cochlea. "Neural" refers to damage to the nerve that takes messages of sound to the brain.

Neural hearing losses may be due to tumors that are close to the nerve that carries sound messages to the brain. If tumors are growing near the brain, the condition is potentially life-threatening.

Other causes of hearing loss: Deafness can also occur as a result of a developmental condition, a disease, an injury, or a genetic disorder.

Developmental deafness: Some people are born deaf as a result of a congenital malformation in the ear. Some are born deaf because their mothers were exposed to the "German" measles virus (rubella). The virus invades the inner ear when the fetus is developing and causes sensorineural hearing loss. Some genetic diseases have deafness as one component.

Deafness from disease: Sensory hearing loss can also be caused by a viral infection after birth. This kind of deafness may occur in just one ear and happen quite suddenly. It is produced by such viral diseases as mumps, measles, chicken pox, influenza, and mononucleosis. In rare cases the vaccines that protect against viral childhood diseases cause hearing loss. In young children, from three months to three years, hearing loss is often associated with a condition called otitis media. Children are more prone to these kinds of infections because the eustachian tubes, which connect the throat with the ears, are shorter and more horizontal in children. A viral or secondary bacterial infection can migrate to the ear, causing painful earaches or hearing loss.

Conductive deafness can be a result of *swimmer's ear,* a bacterial or fungal infection that develops in the ear canal.

Temporary hearing loss may also be due to an inner ear infection centered in the semicircular canals.

Deafness from loud sounds: Sensory loss can be caused by exposure to loud sounds over a long period of time. Anyone who is constantly around loud music, gunfire, aircraft, or heavy machinery is at risk of damaging the sensitive cells that line the cochlea.

Miscellaneous causes: Other causes include injury from wounds or blows, insect bites on the outer ear (pinna), abnormal growths, cysts, compacted earwax, or obstruction by foreign objects. The inner ear can also be affected by allergies or drug use.

Prevention: One preventive step may be taken before birth while others are important for infants and young children.

Before birth: To prevent a common form of congenital deafness, women of childbearing age should be up to date with vaccinations against rubella.

Infants and young children: All respiratory infections should be monitored to prevent earaches and otitis media. Earaches should be treated promptly before any damage is done to the ear by bacterial or viral infection. Auditory screening is often done for children entering school. These hearing tests frequently catch hearing loss that was not previously detected.

People of all ages: Prevention of hearing loss starts with limiting exposure to loud sounds or music. Any sound over 90 decibels is damaging to the inner ear. People who work in a noisy environment should wear protective earplugs. For people who have had ear problems as a result of a punctured eardrum or swimmer's ear, care should be taken when engaging in activities that change the pressure in the ears, such as flying or diving. In flying it is important to keep airways open—yawning helps—so that pressure is equalized from in the mouth as well as from outside. Divers can wear earplugs.

One of the most common causes of temporary hearing loss is blockage of the ear canal due to compacted earwax. Once the earwax is safely removed, hearing is restored.

Relief of symptoms: Injuries to the ear are treated with antibiotics to prevent bacterial infection. Deafness brought on by a viral infection may be treated with steroids, and hearing is usually restored within 10 to 14 days. Physicians usually have special devices that enable them to flush out built-up earwax.

Many partly deaf people, especially those over 65, wear a hearing aid. Hearing aids that help people with conductive hearing loss consist of a microphone to convert sound to electric signals, an amplifier to increase the strength of the signals, a receiver to convert the signals back to sound, and a battery to power the device. People with sensorineural loss may use hearing aids that transmit sound through bone.

Some people with severe nerve damage may be helped by *cochlear implants,* electronic devices inserted into the inner ear to stimulate the remaining nerves in the ear.

For people in whom the nerve to the brain has been severed, an *auditory brain stem implant* has been developed. In this device a microphone, sound processor, and transmitter are placed outside the ear, and an electrode to receive the signals is connected directly to the stem of the auditory nerve in the brain.

Decompression sickness *See* Bends

Dehydration

SYMPTOM

About 55 to 65% of body weight is water, depending on age (infants require more water than adults). Any substantial drop below the normal amount results in the potentially serious medical condition called dehydration.

Parts affected: Every cell in the body contains water. This water contains dissolved materials called electrolytes (ih-LEHK-truh-liytz)—minerals such as sodium and potassium that are required for normal bodily functions. Water is required for transmission of nerve signals, digestion, maintenance of body temperature, and proper blood flow.

Sweating and diarrhea not only remove water but also lower the level of electrolytes in the blood. In serious dehydration the loss of electrolytes results in rapid heartbeat and shock, followed by loss of consciousness.

Emergency Room

Related symptoms: In infants and young children, high fever can cause dehydration. Look for weakness, sleepiness, sunken eyes, and lack of urination. The soft spot at the top of the head can sink. *This is a serious condition. Call the doctor immediately or bring the child to an emergency room.*

Dehydration is often accompanied by excessive thirst, weight loss, and dry mucous membranes.

Ignoring thirst and excessive sweat could lead to heat exhaustion. With heat exhaustion the patient sweats profusely, turns pale, and has cool skin, rapid breathing, and a high pulse rate. The victim may be dazed and confused, but usually remains conscious.

Severe dehydration can result from extreme diarrhea or any other disorder that causes rapid water loss. In extreme cases dehydration can lead to shock and even death.

Associations: Dehydration is a symptom of various disorders that result in excessive fluid loss, including cholera, severe diarrhea, or high fevers. Some of these conditions stimulate vomiting as well as diarrhea, making it difficult to replace lost fluids. Certain medications may promote fluid loss and so lead to dehydration.

Prevention and possible actions: The body routinely loses about five pints of water a day through urination, fecal matter, sweating, and water vapor exhaled during respiration. The fluids people drink combined with water in food usually make up for that loss. Normally a person should drink eight glasses of water a day in addition to the water contained in food.

Coffee or alcoholic drinks, both of which promote urination, are not effective. Administering fluids that contain electrolytes, such as sports drinks, can prevent damage from severe dehydration caused by cholera or other forms of severe diarrhea.

An adequate amount of water is needed for good health at all times, but exercise increases the need for water. Get in the habit of keeping water with you during exercise and drink it during all your breaks.

Delirium tremens

(dih-LIHR-ee-uhm TREE-muhnz)

Delirium tremens, informally known as the DTs, is a serious symptom of alcohol withdrawal. This condition occurs when alcohol has interfered with the operation of brain cells for a long period of time, and the cells fail to return to normal quickly. The DTs are characterized by extreme confusion and hallucinations (seeing things that are not there). A person with the DTs may see and feel tiny creatures crawling all over his or her skin, for example. Delirium tremens also may produce the violent trembling called "the shakes" (*delirium tremens* means "trembling madness").

Delirium tremens typically begins between 6 and 96 hours after a person's last drink, especially after a bout of heavy drinking. The DTs last from a few days to a week or more. The episode usually ends with a deep sleep. The condition is always serious and sometimes fatal.

Although the DTs are typical of alcohol withdrawal, milder symptoms of both hallucination and trembling, especially hand trembling, often occur while alcoholics are still drinking. Unlike delirium tremens, which may cause such a confused state that the person does not recognize where he or she is, the hallucinations of ongoing alcohol abuse may be identified as unreal even as the person experiences them. Auditory hallucinations are often the first. The alcoholic may be convinced that rats are in the walls or that a neighbor is playing music just loud enough to be annoying but not loud enough to identify a tune.

Parts affected: Alcohol affects every system of the body; but the DTs are specific to the brain, resulting from a change in the amount or operation of GABA (gamma-amino butyric acid), one of the main chemicals that controls thought and brain operations (*neurotransmitters*).

Related symptoms: Depression, anxiety, sleeplessness, and malnutrition often precede the DTs. There may be fever, increased heart rate, sweating, and pain in the stomach or chest. In severe cases brain function is so impaired that death results.

Associations: Often chronic alcoholism weakens the liver, leading to cirrhosis and bleeding. Malnutrition connected to alcohol abuse contributes to alcoholic dementia, which stems largely

Avoid alcohol

No food

Call ambulance

from a lack of B vitamins and is initially reversible. However, permanent dementia can result. Convulsions may be fatal.

Prevention and possible actions: *If a person is having an attack of the DTs, call an ambulance or 911. This is a medical emergency!* Do not let the person eat or drink anything, since doctors may have to pump the stomach. Never leave a delirious person alone, even if he or she seems suddenly rational. Relapses into delirium occur suddenly and the person may wander away. Speak softly and calmly. Try to keep the person in a quiet, well-lighted environment with few dark shadows. A detoxification center in a hospital can provide appropriate nutrition, medication, and supervision.

Delusions

SYMPTOM

See also
Alcoholism
Anorexia nervosa
Bipolar disorder
Brain
Delirium tremens
Drug abuse
Fever
Mental illnesses
Multiple-personality syndrome
Obsessive-compulsive disorder
Paranoia
Schizophrenia

A delusion is a belief in something that is not true. Most delusions are so deeply held that no argument will convince the person holding the delusion that the belief is not real.

Parts affected: The cause of a delusion is most often an incorrect transmission from one part of the brain to another. The conscious part of the brain (the mind) interprets the signal, creating an explanation to account for its presence. Because memory informs the mind, the delusion not only reflects the false signal but also the concerns of the person experiencing the delusion.

For example, a common kind of delusion is a feeling of great personal importance, or *grandeur.* A person whose brain puts out a signal of grandeur must interpret that signal based on experience and inclination. For example, if the person believes that Napoleon was especially great, then his mind may conclude that the feeling of grandeur is a result of actually being the grand Napoleon. A milder form is a *referential delusion,* the belief that signs and events are directed especially at the person who holds the delusion.

Many common delusions concern the origin of thoughts, since the mind recognizes that the signal is not quite normal. Such delusions are usually of the mind being controlled by outside forces, such as creatures from other planets or malevolent branches of government.

Related symptoms: One special delusion that often accompanies a feeling of grandeur is that others are trying to inflict harm. This common delusion, which often combines many elements, is called paranoia.

Often signals from the brain are recognized by the mind as coming from the eyes or ears. The mind then interprets these as specific sights and sounds. Such delusions are called *hallucinations.*

Associations: Delusions of grandeur often occur among people with serious mental diseases, such as bipolar disorder or schizophrenia. Hallucinations are common among people with schizophrenia, but they also occur quite often in people with other conditions, notably active alcoholism or the delirium tremens that comes with alcohol withdrawal. Fevers of all kinds may induce hallucinations.

Older people may have delusions that are the primary or only symptom of their mental disease. In addition to paranoia, they may be consumed with unjustified jealousy or develop strongly held beliefs about their own physical state—for example, that they smell so bad that people avoid them.

Hallucinations produced by alcohol, drugs, or fever may be recognized by the hallucinator as sights and sounds that are not really there, or they may be accepted as real.

Anorexia nervosa may involve the delusion that one is fat when she is actually very thin.

Relief of symptoms: Powerful drugs called antipsychotics can often halt the brain signals and dispel the delusions, although these drugs frequently have dangerous or unpleasant side effects. Sometimes electroconvulsive "shock" treatments relieve delusions, at least temporarily.

Dementia

(dih-MEHN-shuh)

SYMPTOM

Dementia is the loss of cognitive skills; these include the ability to reason, memory, and even a sense of place or time. Irreversible dementia is a symptom of progressive brain disease, but dementia often has other causes and may be halted or cured. Though people often associate it with old age, dementia is not an inevitable part of aging—the majority of older people have normal brain function. When dementia occurs among younger people, it is often a result of infection or injury.

Parts affected: Dementia may be induced by various conditions. In progressive diseases, such as Alzheimer's (cause unknown), Creutzfeldt-Jakob disease (a prion infection), or Huntington's disease (a genetic disorder), cells in parts of the brain are destroyed. Stroke or poisonous substances can cause sections of the brain to die. Vitamin deficiency and toxins such as alcohol, drugs, or some medications can interfere with the operation of brain cells without killing them. Certain infections, notably syphilis, HIV (leading to AIDS), and herpes, sometimes enter the brain and cause dementia. Pressure on the brain from such causes as injury, tumor, or aneurysm can also produce dementia, which may be relieved when the pressure is removed. Dementia associated with severe depression may be caused by problems in transmission of signals within the brain.

Related symptoms: Apart from other symptoms related to an underlying disease, dementia typically begins with forgetfulness. As loss of memory progresses, other brain functions begin to falter and increasing confusion sets in. Eventually, the ability to recognize family, friends, and even surroundings is lost.

Vitamin deficiency may cause anemia as well as depression. Some dementia is accompanied by delusions, especially when connected to alcoholism, syphilis, or depression.

Associations: Alzheimer's disease has been found to cause as much as 50% of all cases of dementia in older persons. Narrowing or blockage of arteries supplying the brain with blood, hardening of those arteries, chest infection, heart attack, hypothyroidism, alcoholism, severe depression, and other disorders also can cause dementia.

Prevention and relief of symptoms: Experts estimate that impaired mental function is completely reversible in about 10 to 20% of people over 65. This is because the underlying cause, once found, can be removed. Side effects of medication can usually be reduced or eliminated by changing the medication or dosage. If brain damage from alcoholism is not severe, it is reversible. The actual problem frequently results from B-vitamin deficiency. When alcohol use stops and enough B vitamins are ingested, the dementia ceases. Progressive brain illness, such as Alzheimer's or Huntington's disease, and dementia from advanced alcoholism cannot be reversed.

Dengue fever

(DEHNG-gee)

DISEASE

TYPE: INFECTIOUS (VIRAL)

See also
Animal diseases and humans
Fever
Hemorrhagic fevers
Relapsing fevers
Reye's syndrome
Tropical diseases
Viruses and disease

Also called *breakbone fever,* dengue fever causes such severe pain in the joints that even lying in bed can be agonizing. Despite the pain the fever is usually not fatal. But a form known as *dengue hemorrhagic fever* or *dengue shock syndrome* is much more dangerous and can be fatal in about 1 out of 7 cases, especially among young children.

Cause: The mosquito *Aedes aegypti,* common in warm and tropical climates, carries the disease. It is the same mosquito that spreads yellow fever, but *Aedes* can also become infected with any of the four distinct viruses that cause dengue fever. Infection with one of the viruses does not produce immunity against the others.

Incidence: The southern United States, the Caribbean, and subtropical regions of Asia, the Pacific, and Africa all experience outbreaks of dengue fever from time to time. There are from 50 to 100 million cases each year. The hemorrhagic form is most common in Southeast Asia, where there are several thousand cases annually.

Epidemics of dengue tend to break out at five-year intervals because people who have had dengue fever enjoy a natural immunity that lasts about five years.

Mosquito control programs have significantly reduced the threat of dengue fever epidemics in the southern United States and in Australia, but outbreaks continue to be a serious problem in the Caribbean, the Philippines, Southeast Asia, and East Africa.

Noticeable symptoms: A throbbing headache, pain behind the eyes, and sudden fever mark the first signs of the common form of dengue fever. Some hours later the characteristic back and joint pain begins and body temperature rises quickly, perhaps as high as 106°F. The face becomes flushed and a pink rash appears that turns red as the fever progresses. Severe vomiting and a foul taste also come with dengue fever.

Phone doctor

The pain is tremendous. Even being touched can be unbearable and any slight movement, such as raising a little finger, can be agonizing. *A person experiencing such symptoms should get medical attention as soon as possible.*

Hemorrhagic dengue causes capillaries to burst, producing a deep rash and bleeding from the places where capillaries are close to a thin surface, such as in the nose, the intestines, or the kidneys.

Diagnosis: Dengue fever shares symptoms with a number of diseases, which may make it difficult for a doctor to diagnose correctly. A blood sample will probably be taken.

Treatment options: No cure for dengue fever exists, though vaccines are being researched. Treatment mostly consists of making the patient as comfortable as possible while the disease runs its course. Drinking large amounts of liquids is important. The doctor will probably recommend medications to ease the pain. *Anyone with symptoms of dengue fever should avoid taking aspirin, which may cause serious side effects.*

Avoid aspirin

Stages and progress: The initial onset of pain and fever usually lasts about three days, after which the symptoms disappear. But about 24 hours later, just when it seems that the fever is stopping, the pain and other symptoms return. Lasting about two more days, this second stage brings a red rash that covers the torso and legs. The rash may even cause skin to peel.

Dengue fever usually runs its course in six to seven days and is rarely fatal, except in the hemorrhagic form. But a person's body will be weakened by exhaustion from fighting the disease, and recovery generally comes slowly.

Prevention: The best prevention is through programs aimed at controlling the mosquito responsible for spreading the disease. When out walking in remote or mosquito-infested areas outside the United States where mosquito control is either ineffective or nonexistent, mosquito protection is a must.

| Dental caries | *See* **Tooth decay** |

Dental illnesses and conditions

REFERENCE

See also
Bruxism
Candidiasis
Canker
Cleft lip and palate
Cold sore
Gingivitis
Periodontal disease
Teeth
Toothache
Tooth decay
Trench mouth

Not many years ago people thought they would inevitably lose all their teeth by the time they got old, if not before. But nowadays more and more people go through life with all or most of their natural teeth in good working order. First, scientific research and advances in technology have made it possible for dentists to treat disorders of the teeth and mouth more effectively. Second, more people take good care of their teeth by regularly brushing and flossing. Third, the now almost universal exposure to fluoride supplements—in public water supplies and virtually every brand of toothpaste—has drastically reduced tooth decay.

Infections: Bacterial, viral, or fungal infections may inflame the gums, tongue, or lining of the mouth. One of the most serious is the bacterial infection trench mouth (*Vincent's infection*). Infection by the herpes simplex virus may cause localized cold sores or more extensive inflammation of the mouth. The fungal infection candidiasis often inflames the tongue, causing *glossitis*. Infections are treated with antibiotic, antiviral, or antifungal drugs.

Pyogenic granuloma (PIY-uh-JEHN-ihk GRAAN-yuh-LOH-muh): This is a *benign* (noncancerous) localized growth on the gum caused by inflammation. It develops rapidly, often at the site of a recent injury. Pyogenic granulomas are especially common during pregnancy. They usually subside without treatment but can be surgically removed if necessary.

Gum hyperplasia (HIY-puhr-PLAY-zhuh): Hyperplasia ("overgrowth") of the gums may accompany gingivitis. It may also be caused by severe vitamin C deficiency (scurvy), leukemia, or the antiepilepsy drug *phenytoin*.

Discoloration: Teeth can be discolored by a number of agents:

- *Tetracycline.* The widely used antibiotic tetracycline can stain the developing teeth of infants and children. If taken by the mother during pregnancy, it stains only the primary, or "baby," teeth of a child. If taken by a child up to about age eight, it may stain the permanent teeth.

- *Aging.* Teeth naturally darken in older people because the enamel becomes either thinner or stained.
- *Pulp damage.* If the central pulp of a tooth, containing its blood vessels, becomes damaged, it may bleed into the rest of the tooth, darkening it.
- *Fluorosis* (floo-ROH-sihs). Fluoride offers very valuable protection against tooth decay and is routinely added to the water supply. But in some places the natural concentration of fluoride in water is unusually high, and children who drink it may develop mottled teeth.
- *Silver amalgam.* The most widely used material for filling cavities is an amalgam (mixture) of silver and other metals. Over the years some of the amalgam may dissolve and leak into a surrounding tooth, discoloring it.

Mild staining can sometimes be remedied by mechanical polishing or by applying a bleaching agent, either at home or in a dentist's office. At times a stain can be covered up with a liquid coating (in a process called *bonding*) or with a solid veneer or cap. Amalgam staining can sometimes be reversed by replacing the filling.

Trauma: Teeth may become damaged or lost through trauma (violence or an accident). Slightly chipped teeth can sometimes be remedied simply by contouring—grinding to form a smooth edge or surface. More severe damage can be repaired by rebuilding a tooth with a filling or crown. An artificial crown is a replacement for the natural crown of enamel, which is attached to the ground-down core of a tooth. Knocked-out teeth can often be successfully reimplanted if the treatment is prompt.

Congenital defects of tooth or jaw structure: Both the primary and permanent teeth start to develop before birth. If this development does not take place normally, either the protective enamel or the underlying dentin of the teeth may be weak or discolored. There are several possible causes, ranging from inheritance to maternal infections. If damage is serious, the teeth may need to be covered with protective artificial crowns.

Missing or supernumerary teeth: Many children have either less or more than the normal number of teeth. Sometimes the cause is clearly hereditary, but often it is unknown. Missing

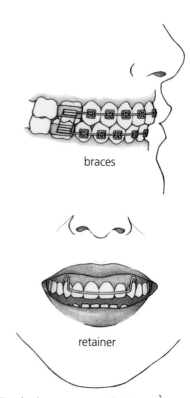

braces

retainer

Teeth that are out of alignment can be straightened by orthodontia. The braces that do this are no longer needed after the teeth are straight.

teeth are especially common—much more so than supernumerary (extra) teeth. Often no treatment is needed unless the condition threatens to cause malocclusion (see below). If necessary, supernumerary teeth can be removed. The gaps caused by missing teeth can be filled with bridges of artificial teeth, attached to sound teeth at each end, or with implants, artificial teeth attached to tooth sockets with metal pins.

Undersized teeth: Many children have individual teeth that are abnormally small. Undersized lateral incisors ("peg incisors") are especially common. Undersized teeth may be unsightly, but they are usually harmless.

Impacted teeth: A tooth may be prevented from erupting normally if it is jammed, or *impacted*, against another tooth. Third molars ("wisdom teeth") are especially likely to be impacted and must often be extracted.

Malocclusion (MAAL-uh-KLOO-zhuhn): Teeth that erupt in perfect alignment are the exception, not the rule. Most people have at least slightly misaligned teeth. When the condition is severe enough, it causes malocclusion ("bad bite"). Often the basic problem lies not in the teeth but in the bones of the jaws, which are mismatched in size or shape. The standard remedy is *orthodontic* treatment, using mechanical devices to alter the jaws, teeth, or both.

Jaw malformations: Less commonly, malformation of the jaws may be so severe that *orthognathic* (OHR-thoh-NAATH-ihk, or "jaw-correcting") surgery is necessary to remedy it. The jaw-bones may be lengthened, reduced, or otherwise reshaped.

Temporomandibular disorders: (TEHM-puh-roh-maan-DIHB-yuh-luhr): The upper and lower jaws are linked by hingelike temporomandibular joints at their ends. Sometimes these joints malfunction, becoming inflamed and sore, or displacing the pad of cartilage between the bones. The cause is often unknown, but habitual clenching or grinding of the teeth (bruxism) is thought to be a major factor.

Glossitis (glo-SIY-tihs): Several conditions cause glossitis, or inflamed tongue. One of them is the fungal infection candidiasis. Other common causes are vitamin and mineral deficiencies.

Depression	*See* **Clinical depression**
Dermatitis	*See* **Eczema; Skin diseases**

Detached retina

(REHT-n-uh)

DISEASE

TYPE: MECHANICAL

Phone doctor

See also
Diabetes mellitus, type I ("juvenile")
Diabetes mellitus, type II ("adult-onset")
Eyes and vision
Macular degeneration

The retina is the light-sensitive surface inside the eyeball. When the retina becomes separated from the underlying layer that supplies it with nourishment, a condition known as detached retina occurs. *A detached retina requires urgent treatment to limit the damage and restore as much lost vision as possible. If not corrected, blindness will result; detached retina never heals itself.*

Cause: A healthy retina fits snugly against the back wall of the eyeball, held in place by a jellylike fluid that fills the intervening space. The normal retina is, in addition, firmly anchored at specific sites. At the center, or *macula*, nerve cells that merge into the optic nerve hold it securely in place. On the edges millions of tiny capillaries bringing oxygen and nutrients to the retina form a bridge to the blood vessels that lace through the layer beneath. Any event that causes the retina to detach from either of these attachment sites and their networks of capillaries and nerve cells can have an immediate and potentially disastrous effect on the eye's ability to see since the cells of the retina die if they do not receive oxygen and nutrients.

Among the relatively rare events that may cause retinal detachment are the opening of a split or tear in the eyeball, an infection, fluid leakage or bleeding, a tumor, a severe blow, a penetrating injury, extreme physical exertion, or some inherited predisposition to detachment. Even the chance formation of the tiniest of holes in the retina can allow fluid to seep behind the membrane, causing the retina to balloon into the vitreous cavity.

Incidence: Detached retina is relatively rare; around the world only about 1 person in 15,000 is ever affected. Those with diabetes and middle-aged persons who are extremely nearsighted are more prone to detached retina than the general population. Persons who have suffered a major injury to the eye—boxers, for example—or who have had some kind of cataract surgery are also at greater risk. An estimated 15% of people who have retinal detachment in one eye will ultimately develop the condition in the other.

Noticeable symptoms: Retinal detachment is completely painless. Often the first sign of trouble is the appearance of an explosive array of light flashes at the edges of vision. The flashes are triggered when the light-sensitive cells of the retina are overstimulated as the tissue begins to tear or detach. Since fragments of blood or pigment are released in the tearing, too, a blizzard of dark specks or larger spots called "floaters" also drift into sight. By themselves the occasional flashes or floaters are not reliable indicators of retinal detachment; only when they persist for hours and come in large numbers or are accompanied by other symptoms is there cause for concern. Often spots and floaters decrease after a few hours or days; but this does not mean that the detached retina is reattaching itself. The condition is actually becoming worse even as the symptoms decrease.

If the detachment is around the outer edges only, some part of peripheral vision may seem blurred or as if in shadow. As long as the center of the retina is unaffected, the sight when looking straight ahead is normal. When the center becomes partly separated, sight becomes distorted, wavy, and unfocused. If the separation reaches the center, or macula, the disruption in sight may be severe; a black "curtain" drops over part or all of vision in the affected eye.

Diagnosis: The detached retina appears higher than it should be and may have a corrugated appearance when viewed with an ophthalmoscope (of-THAAL-muh-SKOHP).

Treatment options: If help is sought very early, and the tear is small, simple fusion with a laser or freezing treatment under local anesthetic may be sufficient to effect a repair. In 90% of cases, however, a more extensive operation under general anesthesia is needed. The surgery begins by strapping the anesthetized patient onto a rotating operating table.

To coax the loose flap back into place the surgeon may use a combination of techniques. To utilize the force of gravity the patient is turned in such a way—standing on the head if necessary—that the flap falls back into position. A puff of air sent through a tiny needle may additionally help move the retina along. A tiny cold probe or a very hot probe or laser is used to spot-weld the rejoined surfaces together. A plastic band, called a buckle, may be attached permanently, or a small bubble may be inserted into the eye to cause the eyeball to press against the retina. The patient typically is able to return to normal activities in a few days. Maximum sight returns in about three months.

For those who suffer some vision loss as the result of retinal detachment there are a variety of optical aids, including high-intensity reading lights, magnifying glasses, and even electronic devices.

Prevention and risk factors: Persons with a family history of retinal detachment or others whose present circumstances put them at higher than average risk should have their eyes examined by an eye specialist regularly to ward off problems.

Those at particular risk include the extremely nearsighted, or myopic. This is because the shape of the myopic eyeball—longer from front to back than normal—puts added tension on the retina. Stretched and thinned over many years, the retinal tissue can be gradually pulled away from its normal anchoring.

People with diabetes are also at higher than normal risk for detached retina. Diabetes tends to damage blood vessels, especially the tiniest among them, the capillaries. Over time the capillary walls weaken or collapse, causing the blood vessels to leak fluid into the spaces between the retina and the anchoring wall behind. Like wallpaper peeling off a damp wall, the retina begins to peel away. The best defense against this kind of retinal detachment is good control of the underlying diabetes.

Developmental disability

DISORDER

TYPE: COMBINATION

People who have a developmental disability have been prevented by physical disorders from attaining intelligence levels expected for healthy persons of the same age. They have a reduced ability to solve problems and to learn new information, often combined with other physical disorders. Another term used in English-speaking nations is *intellectually disabled*.

Cause: The origins of developmental disability vary greatly from individual to individual, ranging from environmental causes such as malnutrition or poisoning of a mother or fetus to diseases that affect a fetus or an infant to physical accidents that damage the brain. In many instances developmental disability results from a genetic disease such as Tay-Sachs syndrome or a chromosomal problem such as Down syndrome.

Incidence: Developmental disability affects about 2% of the population worldwide.

Noticeable symptoms: There is a great range of developmental disability from, at the low end, those who cannot care for themselves and are unable to communicate with others to those whose disability becomes apparent only after spending considerable time with the person. Most of the developmentally disabled are at the high end and can develop skills, including reading and mathematics, to some degree. In between are those who need to live in a structured environment, especially if they have physical disabilities as well as intellectual ones.

Developmental disability does not necessarily affect personality or nonintellectual skills.

While slowness in acquiring speech or motor skills, such as crawling or walking, can indicate developmental disability, the stages of normal growth vary so much from individual to individual that delayed patterns are not necessarily an indication of developmental disability.

Diagnosis: Various forms of intelligence test may be administered depending on the age of the person being tested. These tests often measure a quantity called intelligence quotient, or IQ, which is 100 times the person's test score for mental age divided by the actual, or physical, age. Thus a person who is 12 years old but has the mental capacity of a person who is 6 years old would have an IQ of 100 times 6/12, or 50. Using this criterion, an adult with an IQ of between 50 and 60 is considered to be mildly disabled; one with an IQ between about 35 and 50 is moderately disabled; while an IQ of between 20 and 35 classes one as severely disabled. Below the severely disabled are those who are profoundly disabled.

In addition to intelligence tests conducted by a child psychologist, a pediatrician or psychologist may test hearing, speech, and vision. In some cases it may be advisable to look at brain-wave patterns with an electroencephalograph (EEG).

Treatment options: Most forms of developmental disability cannot be cured, although slow development caused by malnutrition or vitamin deficiency can be overcome if proper foods are supplied early enough. Children who are developmentally disabled benefit from programs designed to increase their ability to deal with real-world problems and from working with teachers who are able to lift skill levels in communication or reading.

Prevention: The steps that can be taken to prevent developmental disability begin with the health of the mother. Proper nutrition is vital—for example, a folic acid deficiency in the mother has been shown to contribute to neural tube defects, such as spina bifida, in the child; these often are accompanied by developmental disability. A mother can also interfere with fetal development by abuse of alcohol or by contracting a disease such as rubella ("German" measles).

Older parents are somewhat more likely to conceive children who have chromosomal abnormalities, especially Down syndrome, that also tend to be accompanied by one degree or another of developmental disability. Tests can reveal this kind of problem before a child is born. A few fetal conditions, such as hydrocephalus will not lead to developmental disability, if corrected surgically soon enough. The genetic condition phenylketonuria requires maintaining a special diet to prevent developmental disability.

Young children who are normal at birth can become developmentally disabled as a result of vitamin-deficiency diseases, such as pellagra, or lead poisoning.

Diabetes insipidus

(DIY-uh-BEE-tihs ihn-SIHP-ih-duhs)

DISEASE

TYPE: HORMONAL

An unrelenting thirst and near constant need to urinate are warning signs of an uncommon but serious medical condition called diabetes insipidus. Unlike diabetes mellitus, which results from problems with insulin, this disorder stems from a deficiency of ADH (antidiuretic hormone), also called vasopressin (VAY-zoh-PREHS-ihn). *Diabetes* is a general term for increased urine production. In insipidus the urine is clear and like water while in mellitus the urine is sugary.

Cause: A head injury, infection, tumor, or radiation damage can all cause the pituitary gland to secrete too little ADH. The

Phone doctor

Drink water

kidneys respond to the unusually low ADH levels by allowing large quantities of water to pass out of the body as urine. The loss of water makes the patient feel very thirsty, but any water taken in to relieve that thirst soon leaves the body as urine.

Nephrogenic (nehf-ruh-JEHN-ihk) *diabetes insipidus* is a rare, inherited condition. Here there is ample ADH, but the kidneys are unable to respond and so pass large quantities of urine.

Noticeable symptoms: Persistent thirst and a near constant need to urinate day and night are the most obvious symptoms. A person with this disorder may have a voracious appetite but nevertheless becomes emaciated and weak. Diabetes insipidus can lead to severe dehydration, although usually the thirsty person drinks enough to keep out of serious danger. See a doctor promptly and continue drinking plenty of fluids in the meantime.

Diagnosis: A physician will take a urine sample to check for very low mineral content and may also restrict fluid intake for eight hours. A well person who is not allowed to drink liquids will soon stop urinating, but a person with diabetes insipidus will continue even without fluid intake.

Treatment options: Drinking a lot of liquids fends off dehydration and is therefore advisable, even though one may associate consumption of liquids with the urination.

A synthetic form of ADH corrects the deficiency. It can be taken as a nasal spray or by injection and lasts for 8 to 20 hours. There are also drugs that can help the kidney respond to ADH in cases of nephrogenic diabetes insipidus.

Diabetes mellitus, type I ("juvenile")
(DIY-uh-BEE-tihs muh-LIY-tuhs)

DISEASE

TYPE: GENETIC;
AUTOIMMUNE

Although diabetes mellitus—named for the overproduction of sugary urine (*mellitus* means "honey-sweet")—was reported by physicians of ancient Greece, it was not until the twentieth century that it began to be understood. Diabetes mellitus, sometimes called "sugar diabetes," stems from defects in the manufacture, delivery, or use of the hormone insulin.

There are two main varieties of diabetes mellitus, known as type I and type II. Type II diabetes mellitus is covered in the entry that follows. Diabetes mellitus that develops during pregnancy and vanishes after childbirth is sometimes labeled type

Damage diabetes does

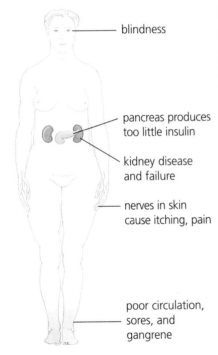

— blindness

pancreas produces too little insulin

kidney disease and failure

nerves in skin cause itching, pain

poor circulation, sores, and gangrene

Although a defect in the pancreas may be the cause of diabetes, the effects are felt throughout the body in damage to nerves, blood vessels, eyes, and kidneys.

III, although it is essentially the same as type II. Damage to the pancreas or side effects of drugs can also produce the symptoms of diabetes mellitus.

Cause: In type I diabetes the pancreas is unable to produce insulin, needed for cells to use glucose as a source of energy. Glucose, the main energy source for the body, builds up in the blood when there is no insulin.

Insulin is normally released into the bloodstream by special cells in the pancreas called *beta cells*. Insulin has many actions throughout the body, mostly connected to energy use, particularly utilization of glucose.

In general the failure of insulin production for type I diabetes comes from the immune system attacking the insulin-producing cells in the pancreas. Therefore type I diabetes is an autoimmune disease, but with a strong hereditary component. Genes are thought to account for about 40 to 50% of the origin of type I.

Incidence: Estimates are that 1.4 to 1.5 million Americans have type I diabetes mellitus, about 1 person out of every 250, making it a common chronic disease. It is most prevalent in people of European descent and tends to appear during childhood or teenage years. Ten to twenty times as many people have type II diabetes, which tends to develop later in life.

Noticeable symptoms: Type I diabetes begins suddenly, usually during childhood or in early adulthood. The most obvious symptom is frequent urination. Usually the afflicted person is hungry but loses weight no matter how much is eaten. A coma from insufficient insulin may occur if no steps to treat or alleviate the disease are taken.

Diagnosis: A urine test or blood test will reveal high levels of the sugar glucose or fat breakdown products, almost certain symptoms of diabetes mellitus.

Stages and progress: After the sudden onset of symptoms, diabetes treated by diet management and insulin injections normally produces no special symptoms, although the victim may tire easily. Treatment of diabetes can lead to hypoglycemia, or low blood sugar, which can produce confusion or a different kind of coma from the *diabetic coma* described below. Over a period of years the disease takes a toll on the body. Long-term complications can include loss of vision, damage to kidneys, and loss of function in nerves that supply skin.

Death from diabetes may come in any number of ways. Among the most direct is diabetic coma. Unable to utilize glucose because of a lack of insulin, a person with type I diabetes may bypass glucose and burn fat directly to produce energy. Waste products of fat-burning can cause loss of consciousness and perhaps death. A more likely cause of death is kidney disease, which strikes 35 to 45% of persons with type I diabetes and 20% of those with type II.

Treatment options: The main treatment for type I diabetes is insulin replacement. Insulin in use today, whether from animal sources or human insulin produced by genetic engineering, is usually injected. Insulin is a protein, which means that it is digested when taken orally—broken down into other chemicals and no longer useful as insulin.

Much research on diabetes has been aimed at improving insulin delivery. Although most injection is done with a needle, one delivery system propels insulin under pressure through the

---

Intensive care at home

An especially successful form of treatment is variously termed *intensive, closely monitored,* or *tight control of diabetes.* Intensive care for diabetes means monitoring blood glucose levels several times a day with a sensitive blood test (not once a day with a urine indicator), adjusting insulin dosage to fit the levels, and injecting proper amounts of insulin four to seven times a day to keep optimum levels.

In 1983 the National Institute of Diabetes and Digestive and Kidney Diseases mounted the Diabetes Control and Complications Trial, a large-scale study of intensive care. Tight control was shown to keep glucose levels low; the control group on conventional therapy had blood glucose levels nearly half again as high as the group in tight care. More importantly, low glucose levels produced measurably fewer complications.

- *Eye disease:* Among those with no eye disease when they entered the study, the risk was 76% less of developing it in the tight care group.
- *Kidney disease:* Of the many complications of diabetes, kidney failure is most serious; it can be life-threatening. Half of the people with type I diabetes develop kidney failure by the time they are in their thirties or early forties. Damage to kidneys was reduced by 40 to 50% as a result of tight care.
- *Nerve disease:* Painful or numbing nerve ailments were found in about 60% fewer patients using intensive treatment.

---

skin as droplets. An alternative to injection that has been explored is administration as a nasal spray, allowing the hormone to pass through thin membranes directly into the bloodstream. In 2001 researchers developed a protective coating that would convey insulin safely through the stomach to the intestine, where it could be absorbed into the blood. But at present needle injection delivers the most insulin to the blood, where it is needed.

Various groups have been trying for a decade to develop an "artificial pancreas," an implantable device that would produce insulin in relation to glucose needs. This, when developed, would eliminate the need for careful monitoring. Some work has been done in relieving diabetes with transplants of fetal pancreatic tissue.

Prevention and precautions: Although not enough is known today to prevent type I diabetes, there are ways to avoid many of the complications of the disease. Careful monitoring (see box) has been proved effective. People with diabetes need to learn the early warning symptoms of having injected too much insulin for their blood-sugar level—nervousness, sweating, headache, and slurred speech—to ward off shock by drinking orange juice or otherwise getting glucose into the blood.

In addition to making sure that there is a supply of sugar available at all times—carrying juice on trips, for example—a person with diabetes needs to check the feet and lower legs daily for any form of sore or damage: Poor circulation can cause the loss of a foot to gangrene.

Because of the dangers of coma and shock, a person with diabetes should wear a medical-alert tag at all times.

Medic alert

Medical research has demonstrated that kidney failure can be postponed or reduced through use of drugs that reduce blood pressure in the interior of the kidneys. The most effective have blocked a hormone called *angiotensin* (AAN-jee-oh-TEHN-sihn), one of the substances the body uses to control blood pressure. Drugs that block the action of angiotensin have been used to treat high blood pressure since the 1990s. Three separate studies showed that two different angiotensin-receptor blockers (losartan and irbesartan) lowered kidney damage as measured in different ways in each study. These drugs do not eliminate all kidney damage caused by high blood pressure, but they postpone serious difficulties.

Diabetes mellitus, type II ("adult-onset")

(DIY-uh-BEE-tihs muh-LIY-tuhs)

Two different diseases are known as diabetes mellitus. Type I (discussed in previous entry, which also includes general information about both diseases) typically first causes symptoms in young people, so it is often labeled "juvenile." The other disease, type II, is known as "adult-onset." But young people can develop type II diabetes as well. Sometimes type I diabetes is called insulin-dependent, and type II diabetes noninsulin-dependent diabetes mellitus (NIDDM). This distinction is even more misleading than classification into "juvenile" and "adult-onset," since many persons with type II diabetes eventually become dependent on insulin.

Cause: In type II diabetes initiation of the disease differs from the loss of insulin production that characterizes type I, but the results are much the same. The basic problem for type II is that cells throughout the body lose some or most of their ability to use insulin.

Type II diabetes often emerges from *insulin-resistance syndrome*, a condition that seems to be triggered by fat, especially fat in the abdomen (such as a "beer belly"). At first this resistance leads the body to produce more insulin, resulting in too much insulin, a harmful condition in itself. But the overproduction of insulin eventually wears down the production mechanism, while resistance grows. Eventually, the body requires more insulin than the pancreas can manufacture to meet the high demand for it caused by insulin resistance. Glucose can no longer be metabolized and the symptoms of diabetes mellitus appear.

Like type I diabetes, type II is at least partly hereditary. A person with two parents who developed diabetes in adulthood has about one chance in three of also developing the disease.

Incidence: Diabetes mellitus is officially the seventh leading cause of death in the United States (after heart disease, cancer, stroke, accident, emphysema, and infectious lung disease). More people are killed as a result of complications of diabetes than the approximately 50,000 whose deaths are directly attributed to the disease in official statistics. An informed guess is that 160,000 persons in the United States die as a result of complications of diabetes each year, making it the fourth leading cause of death instead of the seventh.

Type II diabetes is diagnosed in about 625,000 Americans

each year, a number that has tripled in the past 50 years. Since a person has this condition for life, about 8 million people in the United States are aware that they have type II diabetes. However, it is thought that there are an equal number with the disease who have never been diagnosed.

Type II diabetes affects 5% of the population of the world. An increase in type II diabetes around the world has been linked to a change to a Western diet and lifestyle.

Noticeable symptoms: Often the first sign is an increase in minor infections, such as boils, and a general feeling of fatigue. Frequent urination, which produces excessive thirst, is the most apparent symptom, however. There may be other symptoms, including tingling or numbness in the skin of the hands or feet, blurred vision, impotence in men, or amenorrhea in women. These symptoms usually develop gradually. A urine or blood test may indicate that you have diabetes before any symptoms are noticeable.

Diagnosis: Obesity is often the first clue that tells a doctor to look more closely. The physician looks for decreased sensation in the feet, broken blood vessels in the eyes, and high blood pressure and cholesterol levels. A urine or blood test that reveals excess glucose definitely identifies the disease, often before any symptoms have developed.

Treatment options: Type II diabetes can be controlled in many persons through diet and exercise, but more severe cases may require oral medication that reduces glucose concentrations in blood. If oral medication fails, type II diabetes is treated with insulin injections, providing the body with so much insulin that even poor uptake by cells will capture enough of it.

Careful monitoring of carbohydrates in the diet can keep glucose levels from changing dramatically. Calorie reduction is important also, and should be restricted to 800 to 1,500 a day, depending on overall body size.

One new treatment is a drug that lowers the liver's capacity for producing glucose. The lower glucose level in the blood then reduces other complications. Another drug is designed specifically for those whose glucose levels increase immediately after eating. It reduces the amount of glucose produced from complex carbohydrates by the digestive system.

Stages and progress: Part of the damage from all forms of diabetes mellitus is caused by excess glucose in the blood, but there may be harm caused by other disturbances in the system as well. Long-term complications can include loss of vision from retinopathy (REHT-uhn-AHP-uh-thee) (broken blood vessels in the eyes) or cataracts, damage to kidneys, and loss of function in nerves that supply skin. Blood vessels in the legs and feet become constricted, leading to foot pain, leg and foot cramps, and sores on the feet. Such sores can easily develop gangrene, which can result in amputation of a foot or leg.

Kidney failure develops eventually in type II diabetes, but the patients at risk are typically quite old and many die of other complications first. A third of the 200,000 Americans each year who experience kidney failure also have diabetes. Recent studies suggest that certain medicines that control high blood pressure are effective in postponing kidney failure by several years.

People with either form of diabetes, but especially those with type II, are more likely than most to develop atherosclerosis, and therefore to die from heart attack or stroke. Because both cholesterol and certain fats in the blood easily become elevated, the risk of stroke or heart disease is about double that of a person of the same age who does not have diabetes.

Prevention or risk factors: Type II diabetes is more likely to develop in middle-aged or older people who are overweight or obese, who fail to exercise regularly, or who have parents or other close relatives with diabetes. In addition to maintaining a safe weight with a sensible diet and exercise, have your blood sugar levels tested as part of regular physical checkups after age 40 if you have a family history of the disease.

Diaphragm
(DIY-uh-fraam)

BODY SYSTEM

In addition to having an important role in respiration, the diaphragm is the main dividing wall in the trunk of humans and other mammals.

Size and location: The diaphragm is a partition of muscles and tendons stretching from and attached to the sternum in front, the ribs at the side, and the spinal column at the rear. It is shaped somewhat like a dome. The heart and lungs are above, while the intestines, liver, and other abdominal organs are below. Blood vessels, including the aorta, and the digestive system have passageways through the diaphragm.

Role: Breathing occurs when the volume of air in the lungs is alternatively increased and decreased. The principal agent of change in the volume of the lungs is the diaphragm. When the diaphragm is pulled down or flattened, volume of the chest cavity is increased, causing air to enter the lungs. Air is pushed out of the lungs by relaxation of the chest muscles, including the diaphragm.

Structurally, the diaphragm helps keep the internal organs of the chest and abdomen in place.

Conditions that affect the diaphragm: *Hiatal hernia*—also called *hiatus hernia*—occurs when the stomach pokes through the diaphragm into the chest. It is a frequent cause of **GERD** (gastroesophageal reflux disease), a persistent form of heartburn.

Diaphragmatic hernia is a congenital defect in infants that also allows digestive organs to push through into the chest—usually the intestines. The main impact, however, is on respiration, since the hernia prevents a lung from fully developing. Surgery is needed to put the organs into their proper place and close the hole.

The diaphragm combines with the epiglottis, the flap that closes the air passage to the lungs, to produce *hiccups*. The origin of a hiccup is a muscle spasm in the diaphragm. This spasm sucks air rapidly and uncontrollably toward the lungs, slamming the unprepared epiglottis shut and producing the slight thunk of a hiccup. After long-lasting hiccups the spasms make the diaphragm noticeably sore. Hiccups are most often caused by rapid eating, overeating, spicy foods, or stomach ulcers, but they may also start with incorrect signals produced by damage to part of the brain. Hiccups usually end soon after they start no matter which home remedy is tried, but if hiccups persist, they must be treated by a physician.

A spinal cord injury can prevent the signals for regular breathing to reach the diaphragm. Breathing must be maintained by a mechanical device called a ventilator.

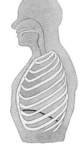

trachea
lungs
thoracic cavity
diaphragm
abdominal cavity

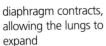

diaphragm contracts, allowing the lungs to expand

diaphragm relaxes, forcing air out of the lungs

Shape changes in the muscular diaphragm power respiration.

Diarrhea

Diarrhea usually occurs when the cells in the lining of the intestines, especially those of the large intestine, are unable to remove water or other fluids from food. Diseases or toxins may kill cells lining the intestines, cells whose function is to pump fluids out of the intestines into the blood. Other diseases damage the lining without killing cells—amebas actually poke holes in the intestines. One common kind of diarrhea, caused by a virus infection, results when channels in cells are kept open, allowing fluids from blood to pour into the intestines. The cells lining the intestines are not themselves damaged, as they are in other forms of diarrhea. Sometimes the main problem is simply excess fluid intake from eating lots of watery fruit, such as peaches, or from high-fiber foods that absorb fluid and prevent it from leaving the intestines. Emotional stress can sometimes initiate diarrhea.

The result of excess fluids, usually combined with irritation from damage to the lining of the intestines, is a watery stool that produces an intense need to evacuate it. The signals for evacuation can sometimes override a person's control of the bowels. Furthermore, in some instances the muscles that squeeze out the fluids push the fluids and any suspended stool material with considerable force.

Parts affected: The large intestine is the primary site of the problem, especially the colon. But diarrhea is often a part of a more general illness affecting the entire digestive tract. In some instances large and small intestines are both inflamed but not the remainder of the digestive tract.

Related symptoms: Although diarrhea is self-limiting in most cases, persistent diarrhea or short-term diarrhea that is very powerful can result in dehydration. Initially this causes listlessness and muscle weakness, but it can be fatal if organs no longer have access to enough water or dissolved substances to operate properly.

When all or most of the digestive tract is involved, diarrhea is accompanied by nausea and vomiting. Dehydration is more rapid when the entire digestive system is affected because of the combined effects of vomiting and loss of appetite along with diarrhea.

Frequently, the same diseases that cause diarrhea also cause fever and muscle weakness.

Cause: Diarrhea is a symptom of many diseases. The most common causes in adults are diseases originating in bacteria or parasites ingested in water or food during travel. Parasites include microscopic amebas and worm infestations of several kinds, including hookworm, whipworm, and tapeworm. Children are more susceptible to viral bacteria than adults.

Reaction to foods, including food allergies and overeating certain foods, is also a major cause of diarrhea. Many people experience diarrhea from lactose intolerance, while others cannot digest other common sugars, including *sucrose* and *fructose*. In some people emotional upset can lead to the condition. Often medicines or other treatments for diseases or disorders produce diarrhea as a side effect. For example, some antibiotics kill normal gut bacteria and allow bacteria that can damage the intestines to proliferate.

Associations: Nearly everyone develops diarrhea at some time during childhood as a result of infection by one of the viruses called *rotaviruses* (ROH-tuh-VIY-ruhs). In developing countries such rotavirus infections lead to perhaps as many as 800,000 to 1 million deaths each year, but childhood diarrhea is rarely fatal in industrialized countries. About 70,000 American children are hospitalized with rotaviral diarrhea each year.

More serious causes of diarrhea include cholera and dysentery, although diarrhea is a symptom of many diseases.

Prevention and possible actions: Travelers, even to industrialized regions, expose themselves to unfamiliar bacteria and parasites that may lead to diarrhea; in less developed regions the diarrhea may be serious. It is generally safer to avoid drinking any water or other liquid that is not bottled or otherwise protected and to skip fresh unpeeled fruits or uncooked vegetables.

If you are traveling to a region where intestinal infections are common, your doctor may prescribe a preventive medicine to reduce the risk of diarrhea. But even if you are taking prescribed medication, you should avoid foods or water that might contain bacteria or parasites.

Blood in the stool requires the immediate attention of a

Phone doctor

Drink water

physician. The diarrhea may be a symptom of ulcerative colitis, cancer, or bacillary dysentery.

Relief of symptoms: For many cases of diarrhea an over-the-counter remedy such as Pepto-Bismol is as effective as more aggressive treatments. Diet can also help—yogurt with active cultures, bananas, and rice all reduce the symptom and may be safely taken together with other treatments. For bacterial diarrhea antibiotics may be helpful but sometimes make the condition worse. Viral diarrhea or chemical food poisoning will usually last for a day or two at most and then disappear. Diarrhea caused by parasites, on the other hand, may persist indefinitely if not treated.

If diarrhea is so severe that you feel you must stay close to a toilet at all times, you may be losing a great deal of body fluid. *Drink large amounts of liquids to prevent dehydration and contact a physician immediately.* Adding small amounts of sugar and a pinch of salt to water helps maintain mineral balance in the body.

Diet and disease

REFERENCE

Disease can be related to diet either negatively (not enough vitamins, for example) or positively, although many connections of diet to health are correctly termed *food fads.* Nutritionists agree that adding or eliminating any single food from the diet, whether it is adding oat bran for fiber or eliminating white sugar to reduce the risk of heart disease, has limited benefits.

The Food Guide Pyramid: The Food Guide Pyramid comprises the official U.S. set of dietary guidelines. The base of the pyramid is the bread, cereal, rice, and pasta group (all made from grains), suggested for 6 to 11 servings each day. The second tier contains both a vegetable group (3 to 5 servings) and a fruit group (2 to 4 servings). Tier three is also divided into two groups, the milk, yogurt, and cheese group (2 to 3 servings) and the meat, poultry, fish, dry beans, eggs, and nuts group (2 to 3 servings). The triangular top tier is the fats, oils, and sweets group (use sparingly). The maximum number of servings is intended for persons with high-energy requirements, such as large teenage boys. The minimum would be for someone with the opposite physical characteristics, such as small elderly women.

Food guide pyramid

The area of each region tells how much of the diet should be based on the foods in that part of the pyramid, from the large base of cereals to the small region of fats and sweets at the top.

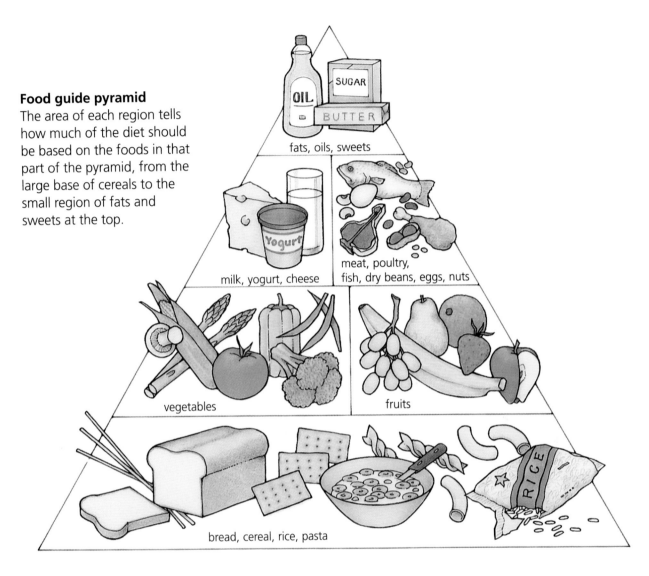

To use the Food Pyramid, it is important to keep servings small. Here are some typical servings suggested by the U.S. Department of Agriculture:

- **grains:** 1 slice bread; 1 ounce ready-to-eat cereal; cup (4 fluid ounces) cooked cereal, cooked rice, or cooked pasta
- **vegetables:** 1 cup raw leafy vegetables; cup other vegetables, cooked or raw; ¾ cup (6 fluid ounces) vegetable juice
- **fruits:** 1 medium apple, banana, or orange; cup chopped, cooked, or canned fruit; ¾ cup (6 fluid ounces) fruit juice
- **dairy:** 1 cup milk or yogurt; 1½ ounces natural cheese; 2 ounces processed cheese

Eat low-fat foods

■ **meats, dry beans, eggs, and nuts:** 2 to 3 ounces cooked meat, poultry, or fish; cup cooked dry beans; 2 eggs; 4 to 6 ounces peanut butter.

Sensible calorie intake: Nutritionists have identified six nutrient types—proteins, carbohydrates, fats, vitamins, minerals, and water—all of which are needed every day. But it is generally agreed that most Americans eat too much—especially too much fat and oil, simple carbohydrates, and foods of little nutritional value ("empty calories"). One of the aims of the Food Pyramid is to reduce fat and empty calories to lower levels.

Sweets and processed food: The foods labeled as containing empty calories tend to be those high in simple sugars or those that have been processed so that fiber, an important part of a nutritional diet, has been removed. Nutritionists recommend multigrain breads in part because of higher fiber content. Cookies or other desserts that are labeled "no fat" often have the same caloric content as similar desserts with fat because more sugar has been added to make them more palatable. Diet drinks do not provide calories, but the people who consume them manage to become overweight from the foods they eat with them. Nutritionists recommend 20 to 35 grams of fiber a day, but a typical American diet contains less than 10 grams.

Dietary fat: In the 1950s scientists discovered that even people who are not noticeably overweight are more likely to have heart disease if they obtain a large portion of their calories from fat. Although the relationship is statistical, careful studies have confirmed that fat is connected to heart disease and to a reduction in the length of life. Most experts think that fat should provide fewer than 30% of the calories in the total diet, and some argue for as low as 10% of the calories. Such low levels do not apply to infants or even to young people under 20, who require a higher level of dietary fat for proper growth.

Fat types differ in their effects on health. The most dangerous for heart disease is known as *saturated fat,* recognizable because it is solid rather than liquid. Another type, *polyunsaturated fat,* includes most oils. Olive oil, which contains *monounsaturated fat,* is generally thought to be better for the heart than either saturated or polyunsaturated fats. Fish oils contain fats classed as *omega-3* and are thought to be beneficial to the heart and circulatory system.

It is not just the type of fat consumed but the fat that stays with you that affects health. Body fat, especially gross obesity, is a factor in diabetes mellitus and suspected in many other ailments.

Cholesterol: Cholesterol is not a fat. It is an animal product that is manufactured from fat, and higher levels of saturated fat usually lead to higher levels of cholesterol in blood. A high level of cholesterol is associated with heart disease. Cholesterol is not found in any fruits or vegetables, even those with high fat content, such as nuts or avocados.

Although Americans are increasingly overweight, they have succeeded in reducing cholesterol levels. This drop in cholesterol levels is part of a 30-year trend that accelerated through the 1980s and early 1990s. At the same time cigarette smoking decreased in popularity and hypertension was lowered through dietary changes or drugs. The result: a 54% decline in heart disease in the United States.

Minerals: Although nutritionists call this group of nutrients minerals, chemists know that they are elements—mostly metals. A few elements, notably calcium and phosphorus, are used in large amounts in hard tissue, such as bones and teeth. Others, such as sodium and potassium, have known importance in maintaining the chemical composition of blood. Some, like iron and molybdenum, are important in specific biochemical molecules. But all of these have many roles, probably in other specific molecules that occur in key reactions. Although the body can eliminate excess amounts of some minerals, such as calcium, most must be consumed in small amounts to be effective. Larger amounts are often harmful or even poisonous.

Calcium: Calcium is useful in preventing osteoporosis, the loss of bone mass that often occurs with aging. Calcium is one of the two food supplements that the U.S. Food and Drug Administration (FDA) allows to make claims for improving health (folic acid is the other).

Chromium: Chromium is involved in the metabolism of sugar and regulation of fat.

Cobalt: This mineral is needed because it is a part of vitamin B_{12}, but it has no other known use.

Copper: Although copper in large amounts is toxic (copper cooking pots are lined with tin or stainless steel), in small amounts it is needed to help form red blood cells, maintain communications in the nervous system, and create normal hair. Copper in appropriate amounts also lowers cholesterol levels.

The genetic disease known as Menkes' syndrome results in low copper levels by interfering with normal transport of the metal across cell membranes. Injections of copper compounds at birth can prevent some of the worst symptoms of the disease.

Fluorine: As a part of the mineral that forms the hardest bones and layers of teeth, fluorine is essential in strengthening bones and preventing tooth decay. Water systems in which natural amounts of fluorides are low often have fluorides added to bring the amount up to four parts per million, a process called fluoridation.

Fluoridation has been in use in the United States since the 1940s, although there has always been some opposition to the practice. There is no evidence that fluoridation of drinking water causes cancer, kidney disease, stomach or digestive problems, infertility, or birth defects. The only known effect besides strengthening teeth and bones is mottling or staining of teeth in about 10% of the exposed population.

Iodine: An essential ingredient in thyroid hormone, iodine, through the hormone, helps regulate energy and promote growth.

Iron: The key mineral in hemoglobin is iron. Lack of iron results in too few effective red blood cells (anemia). Too much iron can occur in persons with a hereditary disorder that causes them to store iron in their organs, where it interferes with function. A number of children have been accidentally poisoned from ingesting iron supplements.

Magnesium: Magnesium is believed to relax blood vessels and thus improve blood flow, but it may also have a role in regulating the heartbeat. Magnesium has helped relieve symptoms of chronic fatigue syndrome; patients with the syndrome have slightly depressed levels of magnesium in their red blood cells when compared with patients without symptoms of the syndrome.

Manganese: Manganese is believed to be necessary for bone formation and health of the nervous system.

Molybdenum: An atom of molybdenum is needed for some enzymes to assume their correct shape.

Potassium and sodium: The two main electrolytes in blood, these metals are needed in large amounts for proper cell function and for nerve operations.

Selenium: Recently selenium has been added to vitamin supplements because it is thought to promote the action of antioxidant vitamins. Some antioxidant vitamins are believed to reduce cell damage that can lead to cancer or heart disease. Selenium is also thought to promote growth.

Zinc: Once thought to be unimportant, zinc is now known to be a part of various enzyme molecules, including some important in sexual development and growth of sperm. Also, zinc appears to be involved in wound healing and the sense of taste. A severe zinc deficiency can lead to short stature and skin disorders. People take zinc to help prevent or recover from the common cold. Physicians are cautious about zinc supplements, however. An overdose can cause nausea, vomiting, and abdominal pains and interfere with the immune system.

Digestive system

BODY SYSTEM

The digestive system consists largely of a pathway for food from the mouth through the body. Along the way nutrients are extracted and waste is carried out of the body. There are also three important ducted, or exocrine, glands that produce fluids for the pathway; these glands are also considered part of the system.

Size and location: The main part of the digestive system is a tube that is nearly 30 feet long, extending from the mouth to the anus. This passage is the *digestive tract.* The widest part of the tract is the stomach; but the stomach is only about 4 inches in diameter, even when filled with its capacity of about a quart and a half of food.

Role: The function of the digestive system is to reduce food to a form that can be absorbed into the body, remove the nutrients, and excrete what is left over. Although the mission is simple, carrying it out requires a long sequence of different steps, with ten or more different organs contributing to the task.

Parts: Thirty-two permanent teeth in an adult (if none have been lost) are used to chop food into small bits. The tongue pushes food mixed with saliva from the salivary glands into a tube called the esophagus that carries the mixture to the stomach. The stomach releases chemicals that break the food into simpler substances, mixing the whole together with a churning motion. As the food passes into the duodenum (DOO-uh-DEE-nuhm), still other chemicals produced by glands are added to the mixture. The liver and pancreas produce these chemicals, called bile and pancreatic fluid. Bile is stored in the gallbladder before it reaches the duodenum. The duodenum leads into the longest part of the digestive system, the 21-foot-long small intestine. The walls of the small intestine absorb most of the nutrients in the food mixture and carry them into the blood.

The digestive system
The digestive system is essentially a single long tube, also called the digestive tract, but the liver, gallbladder, and pancreas are outside the tube, adding digestive fluids to the mix as materials pass by.

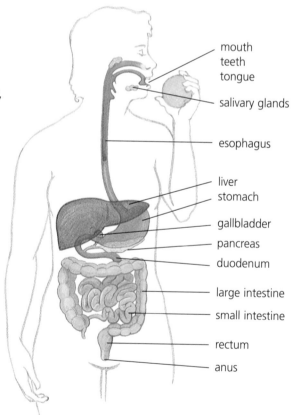

mouth
teeth
tongue

salivary glands

esophagus

liver
stomach

gallbladder

pancreas

duodenum

large intestine

small intestine

rectum

anus

What remains of the mixture passes into the large intestine, where most of the water is removed. The waste collects in a short tube called the rectum. From time to time the waste is excreted through a valve called the anus.

Bacteria, which inhabit the intestines, are not usually thought of as part of the system. But certain friendly bacteria help break down food. If these are lost for some reason, perhaps as a result of antibiotic treatment for a disease caused by different bacteria, digestion is impaired.

Conditions that affect the system: The salivary glands can become infected, most often by the mumps virus, but sometimes by bacteria. The salivary glands rarely may develop small stones or a benign tumor. Stones or tumors can be removed easily by a surgeon. Benign tumors can also affect the tongue.

The tongue and esophagus are also subject to cancerous tumors, which can spread rapidly if not removed or treated early. Such tumors, benign or malignant, are rare. But other parts of the digestive tract are more likely to develop cancer. One possible cause for cancer of the digestive tract is exposure to many different chemicals in food.

Sometimes the valve between the esophagus and the stomach does not close properly. In that case stomach fluids may enter the esophagus and produce the burning sensation known as heartburn or, more seriously, gastroesophageal reflux disease (GERD).

Many events can cause the lining of the digestive tract to become irritated. The most common cause is infection by a virus, a disease commonly called the "flu" although it is different from influenza. When traveling, unfamiliar bacteria or parasites can infect the system, producing the same combination of nausea and diarrhea as the flu. Sometimes chemicals in food are toxic or produce allergic reactions that have the same results as the flu. A much more severe diarrhea, which can be fatal, is caused by the bacteria of typhoid fever or of cholera.

In many persons either the stomach or the duodenum develops sores called ulcers. It is now known that these sores are caused by the action of a specific bacterium.

Conditions that affect the liver or gallbladder interfere with digestion. So does pancreatitis, an inflammation of the pancreas often caused by alcohol.

Colitis affects the lower part of the large intestine, known as the colon. Another common problem is appendicitis, infection of a small fingerlike pouch called the appendix that is attached to the large intestine. Since another name for the intestines is bowel, a tendency for the intestines to overreact to food is called irritable bowel syndrome. When waste fails to pass regularly from the system, the condition is called constipation.

Diphtheria

(dihf-THIHR-ee-uh)

DISEASE

TYPE: INFECTIOUS
(BACTERIAL)

See also
Asphyxia
Bacteria and disease
Epidemics
Sore throat
Vaccination and disease

Phone doctor

Diphtheria is a serious disease that can cause the throat to become so swollen that breathing may be cut off. Thanks to immunization and a thorough understanding of the disease, diphtheria today is almost nonexistent throughout much of the world. But it once ranked near the top of the list of fatal childhood diseases.

Cause: A rod-shaped bacterium, the bacillus *Corynebacterium diphtheriae*, causes the disease. Because this bacterium usually lodges in moist throat membranes, a sneeze or cough expels it along with the usual droplets of moisture. Anything the moisture touches becomes infected—eating utensils, handkerchiefs, clothing, and so forth.

Diphtheria bacteria sometimes contaminate an open cut as a result of direct contact with an object infected by the bacteria. Contact with any discharge from the infected cut may also spread the disease.

Incidence: Now quite rare, diphtheria is most often thought of as a childhood disease. But diphtheria is highly contagious, and past epidemics have shown that adults as well as children can become infected. As with many "childhood diseases," diphtheria is much more serious in adults and is frequently fatal.

Noticeable symptoms: A sore throat, hard cough, fever, headache, and nausea are the most common early signs of diphtheria. As the disease progresses, tissues in the throat, nasal passages, and mouth swell and may begin to make breathing and swallowing difficult. *Get medical attention any time you experience symptoms that involve difficulty in swallowing or breathing.* With diphtheria prompt medical treatment is especially important.

Diagnosis: Grayish or dirty-yellowish patches in a patient's throat are telltale signs of diphtheria. As the disease progresses the discolored patches grow into one continuous membrane and contribute to swelling in the throat.

A physician might well suspect diphtheria at this point but will probably want to eliminate other possible diseases by taking a throat culture.

Treatment options: The diphtheria bacteria themselves do not directly cause the swelling and other symptoms of the disease. Instead they produce toxins that enter the bloodstream and do the damage. The body naturally produces an antitoxin, but as the bacteria multiply, the increasing quantities of toxin can overwhelm the body's defenses. For that reason a key to treating diphtheria successfully is injecting antitoxin to help the patient's body deal with the high toxin levels.

Antibiotics also are used to remove the bacteria. Treatment routinely includes bed rest. Adults are more likely than children to suffer complications from inflammation of the heart muscle—caused by the diphtheria toxins—and so usually require a longer recovery period.

The doctor must resort to more drastic measures if swelling of the throat has progressed to the point where breathing has been partly or completely blocked. He or she may administer oxygen or intubate the patient to facilitate breathing. Intubation involves inserting a small tube into the throat to keep the air passage open.

If swelling is so advanced that it threatens death by asphyxiation, the physician may perform a *tracheotomy* (TRAY-kee-OT-uh-mee). A small slit is cut in the patient's throat below the point of obstruction and a tube that allows breathing to continue is inserted into the slit. This operation has been used to prevent death from diphtheria since 1730.

Prevention: A program to vaccinate babies against diphtheria soon after they are born has proved highly successful in preventing the disease. The first of four separate injections is given when the infant is just six to eight weeks old. Children then get diphtheria booster shots when they reach school age, at age 11 or 12, and at 10-year intervals thereafter.

Diverticular diseases

(DIY-vehr-TIHK-yuh-luhr)

DISEASE

TYPE: UNKNOWN

See also
Large intestine
Peritonitis
Small intestine

Diverticulosis of intestine

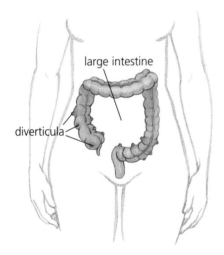

The small pouches called diverticula may form at various sites on the colon. They cause no problems unless they become infected, a condition known as diverticulitis.

Small pouches sometimes develop in the muscular layers of the intestines, particularly the colon (the lower part of the large intestine). If the pouches become infected, there may be pain and bleeding.

Cause: Pouches that form in intestinal walls are called *diverticula*, and the formation of such pouches is called *diverticulosis*. The pouches do not create problems unless they become inflamed, a condition called *diverticulitis*. Inflammation usually occurs when food residues and bacteria become lodged in a pouch. This may result in a small abscess or, more seriously, in a massive infection with rupturing of the intestinal wall followed by general infection of the body cavity, a condition called peritonitis. In some cases openings called *fistulas* (FIHS-chuh-luhz) appear in the intestinal wall, permitting spread of infection.

Incidence: Diverticulosis increases with age and is very common, especially in the United States and other developed countries with high life expectancies and low-fiber diets. The theory is that insufficient fiber results in small, hard stools that put increased pressure on the muscles of the intestinal walls. About one person in five with diverticulosis eventually develops diverticulitis.

Noticeable symptoms: Diverticulosis produces few or no symptoms, although self-limiting rectal bleeding may occur. But if a pouch becomes infected, severe abdominal cramps, especially in the lower left side of the abdomen, and bloody stools may occur. Fever, nausea, and diarrhea or constipation also may be present. *It is important to see a doctor as soon as possible.*

Diagnosis: The doctor will first press the abdomen to see if it is tender, looking especially for pain as pressure is relieved. If diverticulitis is suspected, the next step is likely to be *sigmoidoscopy* (SIHG-moi-DOS-kuh-pee). In this office procedure, an instrument consisting of a tube and light is inserted into the intestine through the anus to allow the doctor to look for the

Phone doctor

High fiber

cause of the problem. A barium enema followed by an x-ray may also be performed to rule out cancer.

Treatment options: To control diverticulosis, the doctor will recommend that you eat more fruits, vegetables, bran, and other sources of fiber.

For diverticulitis hospitalization and intravenous feeding may be necessary. Antibiotics may be prescribed to fight the infection, and a drug such as Demerol may be given to relieve pain. Severe cases of diverticulitis may require surgery.

Dizziness

SYMPTOM

See also
Allergies
Anemias
Blood
Botulism
Head injuries
Hypertension
Meniere's disease
Seasickness

Feeling dizzy does not necessarily mean that something is wrong. However, dizziness can also be a symptom of a disease.

Parts affected: Dizziness is a mental sensation produced by physical changes in the organs of balance. You may feel light-headed or woozy, as if you were about to faint. One kind of dizziness, *vertigo*, may make you feel like the room is spinning or the walls and floors are in motion.

Related symptoms: Dizziness can be accompanied by nausea, just as the sensation of movement in a boat can lead to the nausea that is the main symptom of seasickness. Sometimes the dizzy person becomes very pale, sweats, or feels cold. There may even be loss of consciousness or fainting. In fact dizziness and fainting often go together.

Associations: There are two major reasons why a person becomes dizzy. One is related to the flow of oxygen to the brain. When oxygen is decreased, even momentarily, one can feel light-headed. Thus low blood pressure, which reduces the flow of blood to the brain, or problems in red blood cells that carry oxygen both can be signaled by dizziness.

The other major cause is interference with the sense of balance. The inner ear, or labyrinth, contains three canals that are filled with fluid. This fluid provides one of the main ways that we get our sense of balance. When infections or other problems affect the flow of fluids, the sense of balance is thrown off and vertigo results. Vertigo can be a symptom of a number of diseases of the inner ear, including the following:

Dizziness can sometimes lead to fainting. If you feel faint, sitting with your head between your legs can keep you from losing consciousness by increasing blood flow to the brain.

- *Meniere's disease,* which leads to an increase of the fluids in the inner ear
- *acoustic neuroma* (noo-ROH-muh), a tumor on a nerve in the inner ear
- *labyrinthitis,* a bacterial infection of the inner ear
- *vestibular neuronitis* (veh-STIHB-yuh-luhr NOO-ruh-NIY-tihs), a disease caused by a virus or by small blood clots in the inner ear.

Anything that lowers blood pressure suddenly can cause dizziness, including allergic reactions, botulism, low hormone levels, heart disease, stroke, or internal bleeding. Similarly, interference with the oxygen-carrying capacity of the blood, as in anemia or carbon monoxide poisoning, can also produce dizziness. Some medications, particularly birth control pills and large doses of amphetamines, have dizziness as a side effect. Dizziness may also follow a concussion or violent shock to the brain.

One type of dizziness, called *positional vertigo,* happens when you stand up or turn your head suddenly. In some cases this results from an inner-ear problem, although it may also be caused by blood pressure failing to rise fast enough as a person rises. Some medicines have positional vertigo as a side effect.

When someone faints

People faint or lose consciousness when the supply of blood to the brain is reduced or interrupted. When someone faints, do the following:

- Loosen any tight clothing.
- Make sure the person gets plenty of air.
- Dampen a cloth with cool water and wipe the person's face with it.
- Turn the person's head to the side and wipe his or her mouth out with a clean cloth if vomiting occurs.

People often fall down when they faint. When this happens, the fall can cause serious injury, including damage to the spinal column or broken bones. Movement of the affected part may cause crushing or puncturing of vital organs. It is therefore important not to move a person who has fallen. If there is no serious damage, the person who has fainted can move on return to consciousness. Medical workers are trained to deal safely with people who have fallen.

Phone doctor

Prevention and possible actions: When you feel vertigo, sit still and keep your eyes fixed on an object that is also still. For other forms of dizziness, sit with your head between your knees to increase the blood flow to your brain.

See your physician if your dizziness is particularly bad or if you become dizzy frequently. Also call your physician if dizziness is accompanied by a ringing in your ears, sudden hearing loss, an extremely bad headache, or vision problems. Be sure to let the doctor know about any medications that you are taking or any allergies that may be causing the problem.

Down syndrome

DISORDER

TYPE: GENETIC

See also
Chromosomal abnormalities
**Congenital digestive system
  conditions**
Congenital heart defects
Fragile X syndrome
Genetic diseases
Genome
Hormone disorders
Leukemia

Down syndrome is the most familiar of the genetic birth defects known as chromosomal abnormalities—those that involve an abnormality in the number or form of the chromosomes in a cell nucleus. Many chromosomal abnormalities are fatal, either before birth or shortly after. Compared with these, the abnormality that causes Down syndrome has relatively mild effects. The most characteristic feature of the syndrome is some degree of developmental disability (mental retardation)—usually mild to moderate.

Cause: The nucleus of each body cell contains, instead of the normal 23 pairs of chromosomes, an extra chromosome—one of the pair that biologists call number 21.

Incidence: Down syndrome is one of the most common chromosomal abnormalities, occurring in about 1 out of 800 to 1,000 live births overall. But its frequency, like that of other chromosomal defects, varies according to the age of the mother. The rate is only 1 in 1,250 for women 25 years old, but it rises steeply as women reach their mid thirties. For women 40 or older the rate is 1 birth in 100. For this reason prenatal testing for chromosomal abnormalities is most often offered to pregnant women aged 35 years or over.

Noticeable symptoms: Individuals with Down syndrome usually have a very distinctive look. At least some of these characteristics are likely to be visible at birth:

CHROMOSOMES

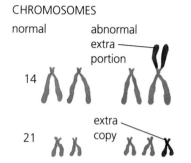

Chromosomes are normally inherited in pairs, one from each parent. The cause of Down syndrome is the inheritance of an extra chromosome number 21. That is, instead of inheriting one chromosome from each parent, the offspring inherits two from one parent and one from the other. In almost all individuals with Down syndrome the extra chromosome forms a *trisomy,* or triplet, of number 21 chromosome instead of the normal pair.

- *small head,* flattened in the back
- *broad, flat face,* with low eyebrow ridges, cheekbones, and nose
- *relatively small ears,* which may fold over at the top
- *relatively small eyes,* turned up at the outer corners, often with a crescent-shaped fold of skin at the inner corner
- *oversize tongue* in a small mouth
- *short stature,* with a short neck, short limbs, and stubby fingers
- *hand abnormalities:* the palm has a "simian crease," a deep, single horizontal line instead of the usual "head" and "heart" lines; the little finger curves inward and has only two segments.

Although this combination signals Down syndrome, similar features may appear individually in someone who is fully normal.

Diagnosis: All chromosomal abnormalities can be diagnosed before or after birth through examination of the chromosomes. Before birth fetal cells are used, usually collected by amniocentesis. Fetal cells are taken through a needle inserted into the amniotic fluid surrounding the fetus. After birth neurological tests can help verify a diagnosis based on physical appearance. If necessary, examination of the chromosomes in a white blood cell from the baby will confirm the diagnosis.

Developmental disability usually becomes evident by early childhood. In addition, a physician may find one or more of the following conditions, either at birth or in early years:

- *congenital malformations* of the heart or gastrointestinal system, which may require surgical repair
- *flabby muscle tone and poor coordination* caused by poor control over the motor nerves
- *hypothyroidism* (inadequate hormone production by the thyroid gland), which slows physical functions and can interfere with normal growth
- *narrow ear canals,* which may make the child susceptible to middle-ear infections or cause partial loss of hearing
- *low resistance to infection*

- *increased risk of leukemia*
- *weak vision*, sometimes accompanied by cataracts
- *misshapen teeth*, with thin enamel

These symptoms, like the degree of developmental disability, vary considerably from person to person.

Treatment options: Until recently, children with Down syndrome had a short life expectancy. More than half died in their first year, usually of infections or heart disease. Such problems still cause a much higher than normal death rate, but modern medicine can now remedy many of them. Heart and gastrointestinal defects, if present, can often be surgically repaired. Bacterial infections can usually be controlled with antibiotics. Viral and fungal infections can often be controlled by drugs as well. Hypothyroidism can be relieved by thyroid hormone supplements. Leukemia, in the form most likely to affect children with Down syndrome, can be successfully treated in most cases. Dental problems can be held in check through early measures against tooth decay, plus orthodontics and restorative dentistry to remedy malocclusion (bad bite) and defective teeth.

With proper medical care life expectancy for adults with Down syndrome is now about 55 years.

Significant progress has been made by dedicated therapists, teachers, and parents in the nurturing and training of children with Down syndrome to help them attain their full potential. In the past such children were commonly institutionalized soon after birth. Now most are raised by their natural families and can expect to lead adult lives that are satisfying and productive.

Drug abuse

DISEASE

TYPE: ADDICTION

If one includes any substance that affects mental perception in any way and that is habituating, not just addictive, then alcohol, nicotine, and even caffeine are drugs. What is considered a drug, however, is to a large extent socially defined. Societies around the world use psychoactive substances, many addictive, in socially sanctioned ways—betel nut, mushrooms, hashish, and so forth. Thus this entry concerns the abuse of drugs that are illegal in the United States today or addictive drugs that that require a physician's prescription. In some cases, however, legal substances, especially inhalants (such as the fumes from some glues), can be abused.

Use of illegal drugs or illegal use of prescription drugs poses serious problems. Mere possession is usually a crime. Because trade in these drugs is illegal, further crimes are often committed by dealers and addicted users to obtain them. The illegal status also leads to practices that can spread disease, including injection with previously used needles and prostitution. Treatment for the drug habit itself, although available, may be avoided partly because admitting to use of these drugs is confessing to a crime.

Because the drugs are often powerful and always unregulated, overdose is a common health hazard. Furthermore, each type of illegal drug presents its own special group of destructive effects.

Stages and progress: Drugs that are abused tend to be those that produce a feeling of euphoria, called a high, or that cause

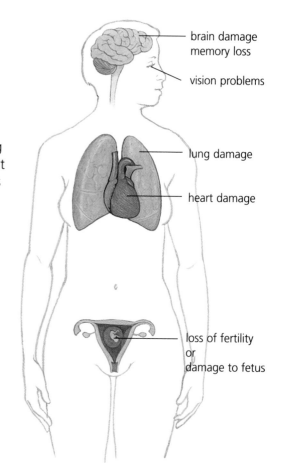

Drug-abuse damage

Depending on the drug abused and the amount of abuse, various forms of health damage may result. All drugs affect the brain, and some may cause permanent mental illness. Use of injected drugs is especially risky, because shared needles often lead to AIDS or to hepatitis B or C.

a dreamlike state that may or may not include euphoria, or that reduce feelings of unhappiness or actual pain.

Drug abuse and addiction often begin with what may seem like harmless experimentation with the more socially acceptable drugs such as marijuana and alcohol. But experimentation is not the only way a drug habit may begin. Often people start taking an addictive drug because a doctor has prescribed it to help them deal with physical or emotional pain. Before long a psychological and physical dependence on the drug develops without the person realizing it. Suddenly, the habit becomes very difficult to stop. When the original prescription runs out, the addicted person may begin a round of deception or crime to continue the drug's use.

Eventually, personal relationships, work, and most other endeavors become secondary to the drug. The addict literally begins living for the drug alone. The longer the person abuses drugs, the more likely that it will become the focus of his or her life.

These experiences lead toward *addiction*—a state that can loosely be defined as physical and mental inability to stop using the drug on a regular basis. Addiction is often defined in terms of what happens when drug use is stopped. Withdrawal from addiction normally produces physical as well as mental symptoms. Another sign of addiction is the need to continually increase the amount of the drug used to create the same high or release.

Cannabis: Marijuana, also called pot or grass, is the most widely used illegal drug. About 1 in 12 youths between the ages of 12 and 17 have used marijuana in any given month. Marijuana and related drugs, such as hashish and bhang, derive from the hemp plant whose scientific name is *Cannabis sativa*. These drugs contain THC, a chemical that usually produces a mild euphoria. Some people experience a panic reaction or other unpleasant effects, however. Hashish, which contains more THC than marijuana, gives a stronger high.

Regular marijuana use alters a person's outlook on life, making the person more self-centered and less concerned with outside events. Among young adults, one study showed, long-term use led to problems with memory and learning, as well as greater rebelliousness, delinquency, and increased tolerance of deviant behavior.

Marijuana can also cause health problems, such as lung

damage when it is smoked (the most common method of intake). Marijuana may also cause temporary loss of fertility, irregular menstrual cycles, and premature births. Withdrawal symptoms are comparatively mild but may include tremors, irritability, vomiting, and diarrhea.

Stimulants: Cocaine, amphetamines, ecstasy, and related drugs all stimulate the nervous system to produce an exciting "rush," or high, for the user. Cocaine and its cousin crack cocaine (cocaine prepared so that it can be smoked; often called crack) are among the most widely used addictive drugs.

Cocaine and crack have been associated with sudden fatal heart attacks. Chronic use of amphetamines, called "speed," as well as cocaine and other stimulants can cause toxic psychosis complete with frightening hallucinations. In some cases the psychosis remains even after drug use is stopped. Methamphetamines cause additional long-term changes in the brain, including impairment of memory and coordination.

Depressants: Called "downers," abused depressants include barbiturates and tranquilizers. Addiction may begin with a physician's prescription, although recreational use of these drugs is common. Because downers produce the opposite effect of stimulants, drug users often take them to counteract a stimulant high. Depressants are highly addictive by themselves; when barbiturates are taken in combination with alcohol, which also depresses the nervous system, the result may be fatal. Withdrawal from depressant addiction can be difficult and if done too quickly can result in convulsions and death. Antidepressants, such as Prozac, are not in this class, and in fact are not considered addictive.

Avoid alcohol

Inhalants: Common household items, such as glue, aerosol sprays, lighter fluid, paint thinner, gasoline, household cleaners, and propane gas are among the thousand or so substances that are being increasingly abused by teenagers. About one teenager in five has inhaled the fumes from one or more of these toxic substances in an effort to get high. The effects may range from mild intoxication to hallucinations, and the risks of long-term use can be severe. The brain, heart, kidneys, and liver all can be damaged. In rare cases "sudden sniffing death" occurs due to cardiac arrest.

Drugs and the brain

A substance acts as a drug when it alters the way that brain cells react and interact with each other. Recent research has centered on chemicals that communicate between one nerve or brain cell and others around it. When a cell is stimulated, it releases one or more of these chemicals, called *neurotransmitters*. Nearby cells that have molecules called *receptors* on their surface change state in response to neurotransmitters locking into their receptors. Some of the best known neurotransmitters are dopamine, serotonin, and norepinephrine. But there are about 60 different neurotransmitters, some of which also have other roles in the body, such as epinephrine and insulin.

Drugs, legal or illegal, work because they use the receptors to simulate the effects of neurotransmitters. For example, there are receptors that cause feelings of pleasure, that produce feelings of sexual orgasm, that cause feelings of satiety, and that relax the body or calm the mind. Drugs use these receptors to produce such feelings artificially, that is, when not stimulated by real events.

Since drugs are not exactly the same as the neurotransmitters they replace, the receptors become adjusted to the drugs and require them instead of the natural chemicals. The number and type of receptors are both powerfully affected by repetition.

Most neurotransmitters and receptors have more than one function. Thus the same system that is involved in producing contentment may also in different circumstances produce unreasoned fear. This kind of interaction leads to drug-induced psychoses.

Hallucinogens: LSD, mescaline, and other psychedelic drugs distort sensations and visual images and otherwise produce a severely altered state of consciousness known as a "trip" that lasts eight hours or more. For many persons an LSD trip begins as an adventure, but it can easily turn into an overwhelming and frightening "bad trip." A single dose of LSD can sometimes cause chronic psychological problems. Heavy use leads to declining ability to engage in abstract thinking, memory loss, and shortened attention span.

Narcotics: Heroin, morphine, codeine, and related drugs, all known as *opiates* (the natural forms are derived from opium), are highly addictive. Heroin users often inject the drug; this produces euphoria and depresses both breathing and heart rate. Heavy use leads to loss of sex drive and various physical disorders. Taking heroin with other sedatives can be fatal, and injecting heroin with a needle previously used by someone else can lead to hepatitis, AIDS, and a host of other serious diseases. Withdrawal from opiates is extremely difficult.

Treatment options: For highly addictive drugs, supervised with-

12-Step meeting

drawal in a medical facility is the safest way to end the addiction because of possible physical problems during withdrawal. Follow-up counseling is necessary to prevent the drug user from going back to drugs. Self-help groups called Narcotics Anonymous, modeled on Alcoholics Anonymous, are useful, but somewhat less successful with drug addiction than with alcoholism.

Duchenne muscular dystrophy

See **Muscular dystrophy**

Dwarfism

See **Short stature**

Dysentery
(DIHS-uhn-TEHR-ee)

DISEASE

TYPE: INFECTIOUS (BACTERIAL OR PARASITIC)

Phone doctor

Dysentery is a general term for various disorders characterized by severe diarrhea, inflamed intestines, and intestinal bleeding. Some forms of dysentery can be mild and clear up quickly by themselves. Others may become severe or continue sporadically for years without treatment. ***Because severe diarrhea can lead to serious dehydration and other problems, get prompt medical treatment for any form of dysentery.*** Dysentery can be especially dangerous for infants, people already suffering other disorders, and the elderly.

Cause: Despite nearly identical symptoms, each of the various forms of dysentery has its own cause, including bacteria, single-celled organisms (protists), viruses, parasitic worms, and certain chemicals.

Bacteria, often of the genus *Shigella*, cause *bacillary* (BAAS-uh-LEH-ree*) dysentery*. These highly infectious bacteria are spread by affected individuals or by carriers who have no outward signs of the disease. You can contract this disease just by touching a contaminated object and then touching your mouth. Eating food or drinking anything contaminated by the bacteria also risks infection. Flies can spread the disease as well. Other bacteria, including some strains of *E. coli*, can pick up the genetic mechanism that causes *Shigella* diarrhea, producing similar symptoms when the intestines become infected.

Amebic dysentery results from infection by the protozoan *Entamoeba histolytica* and spreads through poor sanitation. It is usually contracted by drinking water contaminated with the protozoa or by eating food prepared by people who have the disease. The amebas can be spread in cyst form by houseflies and cockroaches.

Viral diseases, chemical poisoning, or worm infestations that produce diarrhea are often also classed as forms of dysentery.

Incidence: Dysentery was once common in cities and crowded areas throughout the world. Outbreaks of the disease even became a problem at army encampments. Thanks to improved sanitation throughout much of the world, however, the disease is not nearly so prevalent today, although it continues to be widespread in refugee camps.

Noticeable symptoms: Abdominal pain, severe diarrhea, and frequent need to have bowel movements (sometimes as many as 30 to 40 watery discharges a day) are among the most obvious signs of dysentery. There may also be blood and mucus in the stool and a fever. Symptoms are usually more severe with bacillary dysentery than with amebic.

Diagnosis: Other intestinal disorders—such as gastroenteritis and intestinal infections that are less severe than dysentery—also produce bouts of diarrhea. A doctor will check for fever, one sign of a disorder more serious than simple diarrhea, and will look for signs of dehydration caused by the diarrhea. A stool sample will also be tested. If the lab tests find that the stool contains blood or leukocytes, a blood component that appears at sites of inflammation and infection, a stool culture will be taken to see if one of the microbes that causes dysentery is present.

Treatment options: People lose substantial amounts of bodily fluids with severe diarrhea. So the most immediate concern in treating dysentery is preventing dehydration and a resulting imbalance of electrolytes (chemicals such as potassium and chloride in the body that are essential to normal cell function). If you have dysentery, your doctor will want you to drink plenty of fluids. A mix containing water, orange juice, sugar, salt, and baking soda may be prescribed for those who have become dehydrated. Depending on which microbe caused the dysentery, the doctor will also prescribe specific antibiotics or other medicines to hasten recovery.

The reason to mix salt, sugar, and even baking soda into orange juice and drink the fluid is to restore the electrolytes and glucose lost during extensive diarrhea. Salt provides chlorides along with sodium, while baking soda is another source of sodium. Orange juice contains fructose, which enters the blood stream faster than the sucrose from sugar, but both help restore glucose.

For amebic dysentery you may have to take a specific anti-amebic medication. Drug treatment continues for as long as three weeks and you will provide stool samples monthly for several months. Once stool samples show no sign of the protozoa for two to three months, you are cured. Until then, be especially careful to wash your hands whenever you go to the bathroom. This helps prevent the spread of the infection to others and keeps you from reinfecting yourself.

Chemically induced or viral dysentery is generally self-limiting and lasts only a day or two.

Prevention: Good sanitation and safe food handling practices offer the best means of prevention. When traveling to undeveloped countries drink only bottled liquids and exercise care in where and what you eat while there. In addition to avoiding unsterilized water, remember that ice in drinks may be made from infected water and that freezing does not destroy the organisms that cause disease. Similarly, avoid fresh vegetables and unpeeled fruits; not only may these have been washed with infected water, but they may have harbored infectious organisms even before washing.

Earache

When a toddler with a cold tugs at the ear and cries incessantly, it is likely that he or she is complaining of earache, also called *otalgia* (oh-TAAL-jee-uh).

Parts affected: An earache is a pain that can arise from problems with any of the three parts of the ear—outer, middle, or inner. Ear pain may be variously described as dull, burning, sharp, constant, or on and off. The affected person may feel a fullness, pressure, or stuffiness in any part of the ear. An earache can also be *referred pain* that is caused by a disorder in the teeth, tongue, tonsils, jaw, throat, or salivary glands rather than by soreness in the ear itself.

Incidence: Other than scheduled examinations, earache is the symptom that most often leads parents to take a young child to a pediatrician or to the emergency room of a hospital. In the United States this results in about 30 million visits to physicians each year. Ear infections tend to recur. More than a third of all American children have more than three ear infections before the age of four.

Related symptoms: Earache accompanied by fever is likely to be caused by a bacterial or viral infection. Some children also experience irritability, diarrhea, and vomiting with ear infections. Other related symptoms of earache include dizziness and a stiff neck. An earache can be made worse by allergies or sinus infections. Severe earache for which the cause is not properly diagnosed and treated may lead to hearing loss.

Associations: An infection of the middle ear, otitis media, is a very common cause of earache, especially in children under six years old. It usually follows a common cold or respiratory infection during winter or early spring. Ear pain is also associated with *mastoiditis* (MAAS-toid-IY-tuhs), an infection of the bony mastoid cavities near the ear that may occur following otitis media.

Not all earache results from infection. A plugged eustachian (yoo-STAY-shuhn) tube or swelling of the ear canal from any source can cause ear pain. Some people experience earache with *swimmer's ear,* an infection of the outer ear. Another cause of earache not associated with infection is the change in atmospheric pressure experienced when flying or diving. An infrequent cause of earache is a buildup of earwax pushing against the eardrum. Trauma or injury to the ear or jaw may also cause ear pain.

Prevention and possible actions: Young children are the most prone to earache and ear infection because their eustachian tube, which connects the throat with the ear, is very short and horizontal, easing the transfer of microbes from the throat to the ear. In order to prevent ear infection, children recovering from a cold or the flu should be watched for early signs of ear pain. It has also been shown that breast-fed infants have a reduced likelihood of ear infection.

Outer ear disorders such as swimmer's ear can be prevented with use of over-the-counter drugs, which help keep the ear canal dry so that no bacteria or fungus can start an infection.

Another way to prevent infection of the ear is never to use foreign objects in the ear for cleaning.

Relief of symptoms: Use of dry heat or cold compresses may relieve some of the pain of earache, as will use of over-the-counter eardrops. To clear up earache caused by bacterial infection, a physician may drain the ear and prescribe eardrops, decongestants, or pain medication while the infection is being treated with antibiotics. For chronic ear infection the most radical treatment is surgery, but this should be considered only after other treatments have failed.

Treatment to alleviate allergy symptoms or correct dental problems will also relieve earache brought on by allergies or tooth problems.

For earache caused by changes in pressure, simply sucking candy, chewing gum, or yawning to equalize the air pressure on either side of the eardrum helps to reduce discomfort.

Although there are over-the-counter preparations designed to relieve the buildup of earwax, when wax accumulation is great enough to cause an earache, it is best treated by a physician. Most have special instruments that easily and painlessly remove wax buildup no matter how thick and hard the wax may have become.

Eating disorders

See **Anorexia nervosa; Bulimia; Diet and disease**

Ebola

(ee-BOHL-uh)

DISEASE

TYPE: INFECTIOUS (VIRAL)

Ebola, more formally *Ebola hemorrhagic fever,* is a rare but very deadly viral fever first identified in Africa in 1976. Ebola outbreaks among humans have been limited to Africa, but a shipment of monkeys infected with the disease did reach a research laboratory in Virginia in 1989. No humans died from that incident.

Cause: Ebola is caused by one of four long, filamentlike viruses. Ebola occurs in monkeys and chimpanzees as well as in humans.

Researchers do not yet know exactly how the Ebola virus is transmitted to humans, but they suspect it lives in an animal host. The virus can be transmitted person to person by contact with blood or bodily secretions from an infected individual. Doctors do know that once the virus enters a person's bloodstream, the effects are devastating and nearly always deadly. In several outbreaks since the late 1970s, all localized and each involving fewer than 50 people, Ebola has been fatal in 50 to 90% of the cases.

Noticeable symptoms: Illness begins suddenly with Ebola, usually with rapidly worsening headache, fever, weakness, and muscle and joint pain. Within a day or two the disease reaches full force with chest pain, vomiting, diarrhea, and sudden weight loss. Massive bleeding sometimes is a symptom as well—blood in vomit and diarrhea as well as open sores on the lips and even bleeding from the nose and eyes, accompanied by blindness. In fatal cases death usually occurs five or six days after onset.

Diagnosis: Diagnosing Ebola quickly is difficult. The early symptoms are similar to those of many rashes and fevers, and later symptoms resemble other fevers accompanied by bleeding, such as Marburg disease and Lassa fever. Blood samples testing positive for Ebola virus provide the only sure diagnosis.

Treatment: There is no cure for Ebola. Doctors try to reduce the debilitation caused by the symptoms with fluids, oxygen, and prevention of secondary infections. Isolation of Ebola patients and sterilization of needles and other medical tools will prevent others from catching it.

Eclampsia

See **Preeclampsia**

E. coli infection
(EE KOH-liy)

DISEASE

TYPE: FOOD POISONING
(BACTERIAL)

In 1993 four persons in the western United States died and about 700 became ill from eating undercooked hamburgers. It was the first widely recognized outbreak of serious infection by the usually harmless bacterium commonly called *E. coli* (*Escherichia coli* is the full name). Another form of *E. coli* infection, *enteropathogenic E. coli*, is not new; each year diarrhea caused by enteropathogenic *E. coli* kills hundreds of thousands of infants in undeveloped countries.

Cause: The dangerous North American strain is known as O157:H7 *E. coli*. Infection with this disease-causing strain of a usually harmless, common intestinal bacteria results in severe diarrhea and occasional life-threatening kidney disease. The most common source of O157:H7 is undercooked meat. *E. coli* infection is sometimes deadly because this strain has acquired the genes for production of the poison that causes dysentery from a different species of bacterium.

Normally the *E. coli* bacteria responsible for infection live in the intestines of cattle, where they cause no harm. Poor butchering can contaminate meat. Grinding the meat into hamburger spreads the contamination throughout the meat, putting bacteria into the middle of a burger. Thorough cooking can kill the bacteria, but pink meat may remain infected. As few as ten bacteria in one hamburger can quickly populate the intestines of someone who has eaten the burger, producing the serious infection. Less often, other food or water may be contaminated if they have been in physical contact with a source of the bacteria. In one case, unpasteurized juice made from apples that had fallen to the ground contained dangerous levels of virulent *E. coli*, probably from contact with cow manure.

Like other bacterial infections, *E. coli* can be spread from person to person, especially in situations where children are in close physical contact with each other.

Incidence: More than 60 persons per year die from *E. coli* infection in the United States, and an estimated 73,000 become ill. The disease especially affects infants and people over 65.

Noticeable symptoms: At first there is watery diarrhea similar to that produced by a flulike disease or milder forms of food poisoning. When blood begins to appear in the diarrhea, however, there is a possibility of infection by a bacterial strain that produces the Shiga toxin. Any severe diarrhea during a reported outbreak should be viewed with suspicion and treated by a physician.

Diagnosis: Stool samples are tested for the bacterial strain involved.

Treatment options: Specific antibiotics can be used to stem the infection, but there is a problem in using antibiotics with O157:H7 bacteria. Experiments have shown that antibiotics induce a higher rate of release of Shiga toxin, which increases

Phone doctor

Cooking temperatures for safety

The 1993 outbreak had its origin in contaminated meat from six slaughterhouses in the United States and Canada, but proper cooking would have killed the bacteria. Adding 30 seconds to hamburger cooking time stopped the outbreak. The minimum temperature for cooking processed beef (hamburger) recommended today is 140°F, but it is safer to cook hamburger to 160°F.

In general, hamburger or meat loaf should be cooked until no pink shows at all. When there is a choice in a restaurant, medium to well done is acceptable for hamburgers, but medium rare or rare means taking a chance. Rare or medium rare cuts of whole meat, such as steak or roast beef, are not likely to be infected, however, since the interior of these cuts would not have been in contact with the intestines, and the exterior is always cooked thoroughly.

the rate of kidney failure. If there is kidney damage, dialysis may be needed for a time to allow the kidneys to recover.

Stages and progress: In addition to the bloody diarrhea that is the first known and most common symptom, the O157:H7 bacterium releases Shiga toxin that passes through the intestinal wall and is transmitted by blood to other parts of the body. This toxin can cause a form of kidney failure called *hemolytic uremic syndrome* (HUS) in about 10 to 15% of infections, especially in young children, and a bleeding disorder in adults known as thrombocytopenic purpura, as well as anemia. HUS is marked by kidney failure, anemia, and low blood platelet counts. Patients with HUS who appear to be cured as children may go on to have serious kidney problems as adults.

Prevention or risk factors: The primary way to prevent infection is by thorough cooking of foods, especially ground meats, and avoidance of unpasteurized juice or raw fruits and vegetables that may have been in contact with cow manure. Washing all fruits and vegetables that will be consumed raw is important.

History: Workers were surprised when in 1982 an investigation of outbreaks of bloody diarrhea in Oregon and Michigan were traced to a strain of *E. coli* that was infecting people as a result of too-rare hamburgers. The strain, known as O157:H7, was investigated further. Dozens of people developed kidney failure but were saved by kidney dialysis. Similar symptoms were first observed in Switzerland in 1955 but not connected to *E. coli* until 1982.

Ectopic pregnancy

(ehk-TOP-ihk)

DISEASE

TYPE: DEVELOPMENTAL

Ectopic pregnancy

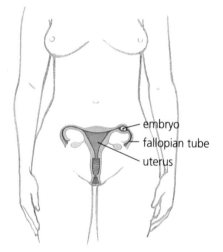

embryo
fallopian tube
uterus

An egg can sometimes be fertilized and the embryo begin development in a fallopian tube, where it cannot develop into a fetus and may threaten the life of the mother.

Phone doctor

Ordinarily, during very early pregnancy the fertilized egg passes through one of the fallopian tubes into the uterus, or womb. There it becomes implanted in the uterus wall, where it begins to grow as an embryo. In about one in fifty pregnancies, however, the egg does not reach the uterus. Instead, it becomes implanted somewhere else, causing an ectopic (out of place) pregnancy. About 95% of ectopic pregnancies occur in the fallopian tubes, hence the name *tubal pregnancies* even though these implantations can occur elsewhere in the abdomen.

Without the support of the uterus the developing fetus cannot survive. But it may grow large enough to rupture the tube, causing dangerous bleeding in the pregnant woman.

Cause: Many experts believe that the fertilized egg gets blocked by some obstruction in the tubal lining. An ectopic pregnancy is more likely to occur if a woman has had a pelvic infection, has undergone abdominal surgery, or has had an earlier ectopic pregnancy. All these conditions can cause scarring of the tubes, and scar tissue may be what interferes with the passage of the egg. In many cases, however, the cause is unknown.

Incidence: About seven in every thousand pregnancies are ectopic. But the rate is rising, probably because of a rise in sexually transmitted diseases, which can cause scarring in the fallopian tubes.

Noticeable symptoms: The first signs of ectopic pregnancy occur in early pregnancy when a woman may not even be aware that she has conceived. She may experience slight brownish bleeding followed by abdominal cramps that can easily be mistaken for a menstrual period. Eventually, though, pain and bleeding, accompanied by dizziness and nausea, are likely to become more severe. *Ectopic pregnancy can be life-threatening if untreated, so a woman of childbearing age with these symptoms should see a physician immediately.*

Diagnosis: Ultrasound examination may reveal an ectopic pregnancy. The condition is also diagnosed by successive measurements of the hormone *hCG*, which increases rapidly during the first weeks of a normal pregnancy but slowly if the pregnancy is ectopic. In rare instances, it may be necessary to examine the internal organs with a laparoscope, a miniature viewing instrument inserted through a small surgical incision into the abdomen.

Treatment options: Sometimes the drug methotrexate can induce abortion of an ectopic pregnancy. But surgery is usually necessary to remove the pregnancy and repair the fallopian tube, if that is where the embryo is lodged.

Outlook: A woman who has had an ectopic pregnancy can have a normal pregnancy afterward. But she runs a slightly higher than normal risk of another ectopic pregnancy.

Eczema
(EK-suh-muh)

DISEASE

TYPE: ALLERGIC

See also
Allergies
Itching
Poison ivy, oak, sumac
Psoriasis
Skin diseases

See also
Embryo
Fallopian tubes
Reproductive system
STD (sexually transmitted diseases)
Uterus

Eczema, also called *atopic dermatitis* (ay-TOP-ihk DUR-muh-TIY-tihs), is a recurrent itchy rash that may first appear in infancy.

Cause: Eczema is an expression of immune system responses in the skin, although in only about a third of the cases does there seem to be a specific allergic trigger. Heat, humidity, or stress may also trigger eczema. The condition tends to run in families and may be hereditary.

Incidence: The most common form is infantile eczema, which may affect 10 to 15% of all children at some point before the age of 5. It is much less common in adults, especially those over the age of 30.

Noticeable symptoms: A child with eczema is likely to have red, chapped, itchy cheeks. Scratching the itch sometimes results in infections that show up as oozing sores on the face and scalp. Older children usually have symptoms that appear in the skin behind elbows and knees. The skin is dry and scaly, appears darker and thicker than the surrounding skin, and itches. In teenagers and adults the symptoms usually spread to the face, neck, and chest.

Diagnosis: A dermatologist can recognize eczema when the patient's history is known, so that other similar rashes can be excluded. Rarely a skin biopsy is used to confirm diagnosis.

Treatment options: Treatment begins with finding ways to avoid inducing the rash. If an allergic response to some food or other substance is known, the person with eczema should avoid contact with the allergen. Similarly, it helps to avoid scratchy or overly warm clothing, to use nonsoap cleansers designed for sensitive skin, and to bathe or shower in lukewarm water.

Using a moisturizing cream on the rash helps—the cream will be more effective if applied at night and covered loosely with plastic wrap. Over-the-counter antihistamines or hydrocortisone cream usually reduce itching when it becomes intense. Long-term use of these medicines is not advisable, however. If the itching is more intense at night, a mild painkiller such as acetaminophen taken at bedtime may help.

A dermatologist can prescribe more powerful medicines that can be used on a regular basis. Also, it is useful to have a dermatologist examine any eczema that does not respond to home treatment, since the skin problem may actually be caused by a different disease, requiring a different treatment.

Edema
(ih-DEE-muh)

SYMPTOM

An abnormal swelling of body tissue caused by the collection of fluid in spaces between the cells is called edema. It may occur for many reasons and may be a symptom of a serious disease.

Parts affected: Edema may develop in three different ways: as a swelling under the skin, as fluid that fills a body cavity such as the abdominal cavity, or within an organ such as the lung. It may be local or widespread.

Related symptoms: Edema may be accompanied by a broad range of other symptoms, depending on the underlying cause.

Associations: Edema can develop as a result of injury, disease, allergy, malnutrition, or pregnancy. Brain edema may be a complication of a head injury. Abdominal edema may signal heart,

Emergency Room

liver, or kidney disease. Eyelid edema may be due to an allergic reaction to eyedrops or cosmetics. Widespread edema may result from heart disease, cirrhosis of the liver, kidney failure, or a severe protein deficiency. Edema that moves—from the face in the morning to the ankles after standing—may signal kidney disease.

Major swelling or unexplained swelling that persists for more than a day should be examined by a doctor as soon as possible. *See a doctor immediately if, in addition to edema, you feel dizzy or have trouble breathing.* The cause may be dangerous fluid in the lungs, or pulmonary edema, which is a medical emergency.

Prevention and possible actions: Diuretics, which are drugs that promote the formation and excretion of urine, are commonly prescribed to treat edema. The doctor may recommend dietary changes—in particular, reduced intake of salt—and bed rest.

For allergic edemas removal of the underlying cause usually is the only treatment needed. If the swelling lasts for more than a day, a corticosteroid cream may be applied to the skin.

Relief of symptoms: Cold-water compresses will relieve eyelid edema and swelling of the hands and fingers; the latter is a common problem among pregnant women. Elevating the legs will relieve edema of the legs and feet, a common problem after prolonged standing. Some medicines, especially those for treating high blood pressure, can lead to edema of the ankles; changing to an alternative prescription usually solves the problem.

Ehrlichiosis (HGE)
(ehr-LIHK-ee-OH-sihs)

DISEASE

TYPE: INFECTIOUS
(BACTERIAL)

Ehrlichiosis—officially known as *human granulocytic* (GRAAN-yuh-loh-SIHT-ihk) *ehrlichiosis* and often called HGE—is a newly discovered disease spread by the same kind of tick that carries Lyme disease. Ehrlichiosis is much more serious, however, and, unlike Lyme disease, has sometimes proven fatal. Often it appears as a coinfection with Lyme disease and sometimes with another newly discovered tick-borne disease, *babesiosis* (buh-BEE-zee-OH-sihs).

Cause: Ehrlichiosis is transmitted to humans by a deer tick infected with a species of rickettsia bacteria from the genus *Ehrlichia.* The bacteria get into the bloodstream when the tick bites. Once there they multiply inside the white blood cells known as granulocytic cells, cells that form an important part of the immune system. Eventually the infection causes a high fever and other symptoms. A slightly different form, carried by dog ticks, is officially *human monocytic* (MON-uh-SIHT-ihk) *ehrlichiosis*, or HME, since it infects different white blood cells, but its effects and treatment are essentially the same as for HGE.

Incidence: First described in 1994, HGE has been found in areas where Lyme disease is common, including such states as Minnesota and Wisconsin in the upper Midwest. HME, although less well known, was discovered about ten years earlier. While the number of confirmed cases of ehrlichiosis is growing, it is still relatively small. In a recent year about 150 cases were positively identified in the United States.

Noticeable symptoms: Symptoms appear in about five to ten days after infection by a tick bite. The person infected may become very sick with high fever, chills, severe headache and muscle aches, vomiting, and lack of appetite. A rash appears in about 20% of cases.

Diagnosis: Because ehrlichiosis shares many symptoms with Lyme disease, Rocky Mountain spotted fever, babesiosis, and other tick-borne diseases, diagnosing this disease can be difficult. Symptoms are usually more severe in ehrlichiosis, however, than in the other diseases, and a blood sample will show a very low white blood cell count.

Treatment options: Two specific antibiotics have proven very effective against ehrlichiosis—doxycycline and tetracycline. If the wrong antibiotics are used, the condition will worsen and increase the danger that the disease could be fatal.

Elephantiasis
(EHL-uh-fuhn-TIY-uh-sihs)

DISEASE

TYPE: INFECTIOUS (PARASITIC)

Lymphatic filariasis (FIHL-uh-RIY-uh-sihs), more commonly called elephantiasis, is a serious disease that can cause legs, arms, and other body parts to swell to several times their normal circumference. A parasitic disease transmitted by mosquitoes, it affects humans, monkeys, and cats and is usually found in tropical climates, where mosquitoes are most numerous. The disease no longer occurs in North America.

Cause: A tiny, white parasitic nematode worm, *Wuchereria bancrofti*, causes elephantiasis by inflaming and blocking off lymph ducts. Related worms, such as *Brugia malayi* and other parasitic nematodes, may also produce elephantiasis. About one and a half to four inches long, these threadlike worms live in human lymph glands and ducts. A male and female pair will remain coiled together there for about seven years.

The worms reproduce by means of tiny larvas, called microfilariae, released by the female. The larvas travel freely throughout the lymph and blood vessels.

Incidence: There are about 120 million people throughout the world who are afflicted with lymphatic filariasis. The disease today is most common in warmer areas of Asia, especially India, China, and Indonesia. Africa also has a high number of cases. It is decreasing in Central and South America and the parts of the Caribbean where it still is found.

Noticeable symptoms: A high fever, headache, and other symptoms resembling those of malaria often accompany the infection. This inflammatory reaction to the presence of the worm also may include the painful swelling of arms, legs, the scrotum in men, and labia in women. ***Get prompt medical attention if you develop such a swelling after traveling in warm regions of Asia, Africa, or Central or South America.***

Phone doctor

Diagnosis: Extreme swelling of the limbs usually does not occur for some years, but a physician can observe inflammation and swelling of the lymph system shortly after an initial infection. The doctor may suspect elephantiasis only if you have recently returned from a country where the disease is common, so it is important to tell the physician about recent travel. Blood tests can confirm the diagnosis.

Treatment options: Various drugs can be used to fight the infection. The drug ivermectin often works in a single dose. Doctors may administer another effective drug, diethylcarbamazine citrate (DEC), over a three- to four-week period. DEC either kills the worm or blocks its ability to reproduce.

Existing significant swelling of body parts cannot be eliminated because even after the worms are killed, the lymph ducts remain blocked. Applying pressure bandages helps reduce swelling on lower limbs. A surgeon can remove some of the extra tissue where substantial swelling has occurred.

Prevention: Drug therapy to kill worms inside their human hosts, along with mosquito control programs, can dramatically decrease the disease in a given area.

Embolism

(EHM-buh-LIHZ-uhm)

DISEASE

TYPE: MECHANICAL

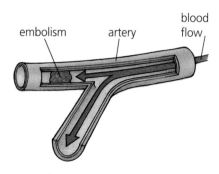

An embolism occurs when a blood clot breaks loose and travels through the arteries until it gets stuck at a narrow part of the blood vessel; then it blocks blood flow past that point.

A piece of fatty tissue called *plaque,* fat, or other bit of material that is carried along in the bloodstream soon causes blood to coagulate around it as a clot, or *embolus* (EHM-buh-luhs). When a clot gets stuck in a blood vessel and forms a blockage, the obstruction is called an embolism.

Cause: Blood clots form for a variety of reasons. Usually a clot forms inside a blood vessel at a place where there is a buildup of plaque. At other times a bit of fat or plaque breaks off the lining of an artery, and a drifting clot forms around it.

Clot formation is also stimulated by inflammation of a vein or damage to a vein lining from an infection or injury. In addition, surgery can initiate embolisms.

Blood circulation can become very sluggish in people who are not actively moving around—for example, people recovering from surgery or sitting still on long airplane flights. Their blood is more likely to coagulate, or clot. One result is *deep-vein thrombosis* (throm-BOH-sihs), typically the formation of a clot in deep veins of the calf, or lower leg. These clots can break off and move to form embolisms in other parts of the body.

Incidence: Blood clots with associated embolisms affect millions of Americans every year. About half a million of these incidents are considered serious enough to be dangerous. *Pulmonary embolism,* which often starts with deep-vein thrombosis, is a dangerous disorder caused by a clot in the artery between the heart and lungs. It strikes half a million Americans each year, causing about 50,000 deaths. Strokes caused by embolisms reach another half million Americans, but cause 150,000 deaths. Both pulmonary embolism and stroke affect half again as many women as men.

Phone doctor

Call ambulance

Emergency Room

Blood clots are more common among people with certain other conditions, such as diabetes or any form of heart disease, including atrial fibrillation, endocarditis, heart failure, or problems with blood circulation. Clots are more likely to occur in people who are older or overweight. All smokers, especially women who smoke and also take birth control pills, are at risk.

Noticeable symptoms: An embolism in an arm or leg may cause pain or tingling in the limb. If it is not treated, the limb may become weak or numb and turn blue from lack of oxygen. Deep-vein thrombosis in the leg may cause the leg to become very painful and swollen. See your physician for these symptoms, especially since a deep-vein clot may cause pulmonary embolism.

If pulmonary embolism strikes, you will feel breathless and perhaps have chest pain. You may cough up blood and feel faint. If this happens, ***get medical assistance immediately.***

An embolism in a coronary artery is the most common cause of a heart attack. An embolism that blocks the flow of blood to the brain is one of the main causes of stroke. (See separate articles on these conditions for symptoms.) Both heart attacks and strokes are medical emergencies. ***An ambulance and your physician should be called immediately.***

If you suddenly lose all or part of your vision in one eye, it may be due to an embolism blocking the artery that brings blood to the retina. ***Emergency treatment is required.***

Diagnosis: Your physician will probably do various tests to find the exact location of the embolism. The physician will also want to determine how much damage has been done to affected tissues and organs.

Regular x-ray images may be taken or you may have an ultrasound scan. The physician may decide to use *magnetic resonance imaging,* or MRI, to located and to assess an embolism. MRI uses strong magnets to form three-dimensional pictures of the brain, lungs, heart, or other parts of the body.

If necessary, another procedure called *angiography* (AAN-jee-OG-ruh-fee) may be employed. A narrow tube is inserted into an artery or vein; then a dye is injected into the tube. As the dye works its way through the blood vessels, it shows up on x-ray images.

Treatment options: Drugs are commonly used as an immediate treatment for embolism. *Anticoagulants* (AAN-tee-koh-AAG-yuh-luhntz) such as heparin or warfarin (Coumadin) are used to prevent clots from forming. Aspirin, working by a different mechanism, also helps prevent clot formation. Sometimes more expensive *thrombolytic* (THROM-boh-LIHT-ihk) *drugs*, primarily streptokinase or t-PA (tissue plasminogen activator), are used to encourage the body's natural processes to break up or dissolve an already formed clot.

If drugs do not work to dissolve a clot that is in a blood vessel, surgery is usually required. A tube is inserted into the artery, and the clot is sucked out mechanically. A person who has had a heart attack or stroke due to an embolism may need more serious surgery.

Prevention: Many people, because of their age, hypertension, or heart disease, take a low dose of aspirin, such as a "baby aspirin" or "regimen aspirin" (81 mg each), every day or every other day. Aspirin makes the blood less sticky and reduces the likelihood of clotting. However, aspirin taken regularly can have serious side effects. Use it every day only if prescribed by a doctor. Those who have atrial fibrillation usually take a stronger anticoagulant daily, typically warfarin. The dosage needs to be carefully monitored by a physician as the margin between preventing blood clots and causing internal bleeding is narrow.

Tobacco, cocaine, and certain other drugs cause the blood to become sticky. In addition to other reasons for avoiding these substances, they should be shunned because of the danger of blood clots. Women who take birth control pills have a slightly greater risk for embolism, which is further increased by tobacco use.

Sitting for a long time in a car or on an airplane can slow blood circulation. Do simple exercises with the feet and legs while sitting. Try to get up and move around at frequent intervals. People recovering from an illness or surgery should get up and move about as soon as they can do so to prevent circulation problems.

Don't smoke

Exercise

Embryo

(EHM-bree-OH)

BODY SYSTEM

See also
Birth canal
Childbirth, complications of
Ectopic pregnancy
Fallopian tubes
Fetus
Genetic diseases
Pregnancy and disease
Reproductive system
Stem cells
Uterus

The developing fetus

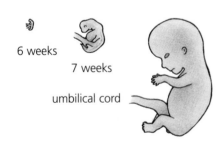

6 weeks

7 weeks

umbilical cord

Although the developing fetus is still quite small at two or three months, it has reached the point where a human shape can easily be seen.

The embryo is a very early stage in the development of a new individual, but people from different medical and scientific specialties use the word to mean slightly different stages.

Although many people would say that an individual is conceived as soon as an ovum (egg) is fertilized by a sperm cell, the fertilized egg is called a *zygote* (ZIY-goht), not an embryo. When a zygote divides into a pair of joined cells, the organism begins to be called an embryo by workers in the field of in vitro fertilization (also called "test tube fertilization"), but not by most biologists. During in vitro fertilization or storage before implantation a zygote that has grown to a number of cells that would make it a candidate for implantation in a prospective mother (usually 32 cells) continues to be called an embryo. At this early stage, however, the small group of cells is called a *blastocyst* (BLAAS-tuh-sihst) by most biologists.

When a mammalian blastocyst implants itself in the uterine wall, it is called an embryo by biologists and by all physicians. After implantation in the uterus the growing cell mass continues to be known as an embryo for several weeks. After the shape of the new individual begins to emerge and organs begin to develop, the term *fetus* is introduced—usually at around eight weeks. The developing baby is then known as a fetus until birth.

Size and location: An embryo is barely visible as a speck at first, when it has just lodged in the uterine wall. There it grows for a month or two to become an inch or two long. At that time, when the embryo has become a fetus, the uterus has swollen, making it possible to feel a slight bulge through the abdominal wall of the mother-to-be.

Role: The first stage of development occurs in the zygote, when some internal separation of cell parts and material occurs before the first division into two cells. As a result, the two cells in the first stage of the blastocyst are different from each other. These differences cause further cells to be individualized in their structure and operation, leading eventually to the specialized tissues of the fetus. *Embryonic stem cells* are cells that still have the potential to develop into almost any kind of cell in the adult.

Conditions that affect the embryo: Because the entire plan of development depends on correct differentiation of cells in early stages, an error in embryonic development usually leads to natural abortion, commonly called *miscarriage* (also called spontaneous abortion). Natural abortion is common; one estimate is that miscarriage occurs in three out of ten pregnancies. The defective embryo is expelled, and pregnancy is terminated, usually with no harm to the pregnant woman. However, complications can occur if part of the embryo or the placenta, the organ that develops to connect the embryo to its mother, remains in the uterus. *Save solid materials expelled during a miscarriage for a physician to examine.* If there is evidence that some tissue has not been expelled, the physician will perform a simple procedure to remove the rest.

Sometimes the embryo fails to implant in the uterine wall but continues to develop in a different location, most often one of the tubes that connect the ovaries to the uterus. This situation is called an ectopic pregnancy. No signs of pregnancy appear, but abdominal pain continues hour after hour. *Abdominal pain in a woman of childbearing age requires immediate medical assistance.*

Emergency Room

Emerging diseases

REFERENCE

The Centers for Disease Control and Prevention (CDC) is the United States' public health department. It defines *emerging infectious disease* as any disease caused by an infectious agent that has increased during the last 20 years or that threatens to increase in the future. There are many illnesses that fit the description.

- Diseases that were thought to be under control, or even conquered, have returned. Since the mid-1980s tuberculosis has been on the rise. In the early 1990s there was a large outbreak of measles.
- New diseases have appeared or have been discovered. AIDS and Lyme disease may be the most familiar new or newly recognized diseases, but other, less well known, diseases are also present. The first case of *babesiosis*, a parasitic disease carried by ticks, was reported from Nantucket Island, Massachusetts, in 1969. Ehrlichiosis, discovered in the late 1980s, is a sometimes fatal bacterial disease that is also transmitted by ticks. The hantavirus transmitted through the droppings

of infected mice, which causes severe, often fatal respiratory problems, was not recognized until 1993. The animal disease *bovine spongiform encephalitis*, known as mad cow disease, appeared in England in the 1990s and was followed by a prion-caused disease in humans produced by contact with beef from cattle infected with mad cow disease.

■ Diseases once seen only outside of the United States have arrived on its shores. Malaria is on the increase in the United States and West Nile encephalitis reached North America in 1999 and since has resulted in nine deaths.

■ Publicity can make a rare disease suddenly seem like an epidemic. "Staph" infections of one kind became famous as "flesh-eating bacteria," while another kind, linked to use of a type of tampon, gained notoriety as toxic shock syndrome.

Why are we seeing emerging diseases? Many factors contribute to emerging diseases.

Social changes: War and poverty reduce access to nutritious food, clean water, and medical care and may cause people to flee their own countries, bringing diseases with them. Since 1980 many people from Asia and Central and South America have immigrated to the United States. In these parts of the world large numbers of people have tuberculosis germs in their bodies, but are not sick. In a new environment and under a lot of stress some of these new immigrants have become sick from the tuberculosis germs already in their bodies. Other people, especially those with weakened immune systems, catch the disease from these sources.

International travel is now taken for granted, with millions of people flying from one continent to another each year. On these trips many people have returned with a disease in addition to snapshots of their travels.

With more mothers working, more children are in day care than ever before. Because young children have not learned adult bathroom habits, day-care centers frequently have outbreaks of diseases of the intestinal tract that can spread from dirty diapers, including hepatitis A, *E. coli* 0157:H7 and *Shigella* infections, giardia, and cryptosporidiosis.

Health care: Antibiotics were once considered wonder drugs because they were so effective in killing bacteria. Now many bacteria are resistant to the very drugs that once killed them. Drug-resistant tuberculosis no longer responds to the drugs that have the fewest side effects and that had in the past been most effective against the disease. Drug-resistant forms of gonorrhea, staph infections, and pneumococcal infections can result in ear infections, pneumonia, and meningitis. Although resistant bacteria have been the biggest problem, some viruses, fungi, and parasites that cause disease have also become unresponsive to the drugs used to fight them.

The widespread use of blood transfusions has sometimes spread disease, most noticeably hepatitis C in recent years. In general when it is discovered that blood transfusions, organ transplants, or use of medicines derived from human tissues are spreading a disease, tests are quickly created to eliminate the infected material from the pipeline.

Food production: Food handling and processing are regulated to protect the public from diseases transmitted through foods. But no system is perfect, and problems sometimes occur. In most large cities you can buy fresh produce and seafood from exotic places all year long. A party in the late 1990s resulted in many guests with food poisoning. The illness was traced back to fresh imported raspberries contaminated with the bacterium *Cyclospora*.

Animals that are routinely given antibiotics tend to grow faster and larger. This practice, however, has been shown to result in humans being infected with antibiotic-resistant strains of bacteria.

Environmental changes: Natural forces, natural disasters, and human activity constantly change the landscape. These changes can provide an ideal setting for emerging diseases.

The improvement of farming methods has led to many former fields being allowed to return to forest, especially in the American Northeast. The still immature forest creates a desirable habitat for deer and the deer ticks that carry Lyme disease, ehrlichiosis, and babesiosis. When humans come into the reforested area for recreation, some become infected with these diseases.

After almost a century of absence cholera returned to the western hemisphere in the early 1990s in an epidemic that spread through South and Central America and into Mexico. In 1992 an especially dangerous variant of the cholera bacterium, *Vibrio cholerae* O139, was discovered in India. The exact cause of the outbreaks is uncertain since cholera epidemics have occurred several times in the past, but environmental changes related to global warming are considered to be a cause. Similarly, global warming may be a factor in the spread north and south of diseases associated primarily with the tropics, such as malaria and dengue fever, both carried by mosquitoes.

Public health successes: During the 1970s and 1980s there was a dramatic decrease in diseases prevented by vaccination. Measles, rubella, and whooping cough seemed to be diseases that were no longer a problem. Then measles outbreaks began to occur, especially on college campuses. Two factors contributed. One was the discovery that measles vaccination does not last forever. Many of those affected had been vaccinated as babies but were now in their twenties. The other factor was the finding that many school-aged children had not been properly immunized against measles in the first place. In other countries there were similar developments. In Russia, for example, a small diphtheria epidemic followed lowered standards for vaccination against the disease.

Most areas of the United States conducted mosquito-control programs to prevent diseases transmitted by mosquitoes. But by the 1970s there were few cases of these diseases, so many programs were abandoned. Then in 1999 in the New York City area people became ill with West Nile encephalitis, which is transmitted by the bite of an infected mosquito.

Bioterrorism: One form of bioterrorism is the deliberate release of disease-causing microorganisms to harm people. The microbes of choice are anthrax and smallpox.

Anthrax is rare in the United States, and few people have been vaccinated for it. In addition, it is easy to grow and disperse anthrax spores. These characteristics make anthrax and smallpox attractive to people who want to terrorize others with biological weapons. Late in 2001 anthrax spores sent through the mail succeeded in causing several deaths and even more fear and anxiety.

In 1980 the World Health Organization proclaimed that since 1977 smallpox had been eliminated as a disease. The only smallpox viruses that remain are supposed to be cultures in laboratories. Most people are no longer vaccinated against smallpox, and those who were vaccinated as children have probably outlived the protection of the vaccine. Some believe that terrorists may find access to a supply of the smallpox virus. In response, governments are stockpiling vaccine (which is based on a different virus) and even considering reintroducing routine smallpox vaccination.

How do we protect against emerging diseases? Individuals can stay informed about disease outbreaks and prevention and make the best health decisions their information allows. Keep immunizations up to date. As new vaccines become available, discuss with your doctor whether you should be vaccinated. Take antibiotics only for bacterial infections and only when they are required. Take all medication exactly as it is prescribed. Learn about diseases you might be exposed to and how to prevent them.

Institutions such as hospitals and public health agencies have an important job in protecting against emerging diseases. Cases of infectious diseases must be reported to local, state, and federal public health departments. This reporting allows health departments to see when a new disease or an outbreak of a known disease occurs. Such disease surveillance helps health officials find the source of infection and locate individuals who might have been exposed. One of the most important things health departments do when there is an emerging disease is to provide good, accurate information so citizens know how to protect themselves.

Emphysema

(EHM-fih-SEE-muh)

DISEASE

TYPE: MECHANICAL; CHEMICAL; GENETIC

Emphysema is a debilitating and often fatal disease that develops when lung tissue has been seriously damaged. People who smoke heavily all their lives may very likely develop emphysema if other illnesses caused by smoking have not already shortened their lives. Emphysema may also have other causes than smoking. Hereditary emphysema sometimes develops in children, and age-related emphysema occurs occasionally in older people, especially those who have been sedentary for much of their lives.

Cause: Under normal conditions fresh air and air laden with carbon dioxide both move freely through the main airways in the lungs, the *bronchi* (BRONG-kiy), and the *bronchioles* (BRONG-kee-OHLZ). At the ends of the bronchioles are clusters of tiny air sacs called *alveoli* (aal-VEE-uh-LIY). It is in the alveoli that the exchange of oxygen and carbon dioxide takes place. When the air passages are continually swollen and clogged, the alveoli may swell and burst. A person who has many swollen or damaged alveoli has emphysema.

Smoking and air pollution are important factors in the development of emphysema. The production of mucus in the airways is increased by smoking or air pollutants, which cause bronchial passages to become inflamed and swollen.

Emphysema is often associated with chronic bronchitis. Asthma attacks and tuberculosis can also produce inflamed and swollen breathing passages that are filled with mucus.

Emphysema tends to damage the small blood vessels of the lungs, gradually causing the heart to work harder in pumping blood through the lungs. This extra work may result in right-sided heart failure.

Acute emphysema can be caused by any episode of labored breathing that ruptures alveoli, including asphyxia (suffocation). In a relatively small number of cases emphysema develops because of an inherited lack of a body chemical that ordinarily helps prevent the destruction of lung tissue.

Incidence and risk factors: Emphysema causes most American deaths from respiratory disease. Three-fifths of the 2 million Americans with the disease are men over the age of 45 who have

Effects of emphysema

Although the damage in emphysema is to the smallest part of the lungs, the alveoli, those tiny pockets are where the real work of respiration takes place.

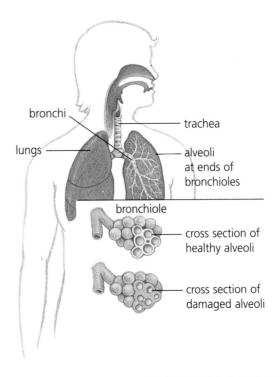

bronchi

trachea

lungs

alveoli
at ends of
bronchioles

bronchiole

cross section of
healthy alveoli

cross section of
damaged alveoli

been heavy smokers; but since more women have taken up smoking, there has been an increase in the incidence of emphysema in women. Nine out of ten persons with emphysema develop the disease from smoking, but others at risk live in urban areas with heavily polluted air or use the lungs in strenuous activities such as glassblowing or playing wind instruments.

Noticeable symptoms: The disease often begins as chronic bronchitis with frequent colds and heavy coughing. Breathing difficulties may be relatively infrequent at first, occurring only when walking, climbing stairs, or doing some other vigorous activity. Later, even moderate exertion brings on *shortness of breath*, a condition in which a person cannot get enough air into the lungs, and must take fast, shallow breaths. Eventually, breathing may be an effort even when resting or lying down. There may be unequal chest expansion if one lung is more affected than the other. Flulike symptoms, such as fever, weakness, and fatigue, are possible. In advanced cases mental problems caused by low oxygen and high carbon dioxide may include dementia as well as symptoms of depression.

In the later stages of emphysema breathing becomes more and more difficult. Breathing may be even more difficult while lying down, resulting in lack of sleep. Shortness of breath leads to blue-tone skin, rapid heartbeat, and a feeling of doom, all similar symptoms to those of heart disease: In both cases the symptoms are caused by lack of oxygen and excess carbon dioxide. ***Recurring breathlessness should be brought to the attention of a physician.***

Diagnosis: During a routine examination or when shortness of breath is reported, a physician will probably ask the patient to perform simple tests that measure lung capacity. The physician will use various other tests to determine whether emphysema is the cause of shortness of breath, if detected. A stethoscope will be used to listen to the heart and lungs. The physician will also place two fingers on the patient's chest and tap them with the fingers of the other hand. If the alveoli have been stretched and enlarged, they will produce a hollow sound when tapped. A chest x-ray and measurements of oxygen in the blood will help assess lung damage.

Treatment options: Lung damage caused by emphysema cannot be reversed. There are, however, some steps one can take to relieve symptoms and to prevent additional complications.

Phone doctor

Don't smoke

Exercise

Rest

Drink water

Smokers must give up the practice completely. A physician may recommend that a person living in an area of heavy air pollution move to a region with cleaner air.

A physician may prescribe medication that will prevent inflammation or widen breathing passages. Often these drugs are administered with an aerosol inhaler or a nebulizer. Antibiotics help prevent respiratory infection. In later stages a person with emphysema may have to use supplemental oxygen continuously or perhaps only at certain times of the day or night.

Exercise can strengthen the diaphragm and abdominal muscles, often easing breathing. It is also important to exercise the rest of the body as part of a regular program. Lack of physical activity can result in general disability.

A person with emphysema needs to schedule regular rest periods during the day. There are specific positions to take when lying down that avoid mucus buildup in the lungs and air passages. Drinking two or three quarts of fluid each day also helps relieve symptoms.

The most severe cases of emphysema may require a lung transplant or a heart/lung transplant.

Prevention: The best prevention is to avoid smoking and air pollution. Immunization against such diseases as influenza or pneumonia is an important protection. Lung infections need to be treated early by a physician, especially if they involve heavy coughing, constricted airways, or fluid in the lungs.

Encephalitis

(ehn-SEHF-uh-LIY-tihs)

DISEASE AND SYMPTOM

TYPE: INFECTIOUS (VIRAL); CHEMICAL

Encephalitis is an inflammation of the brain, which leads to swelling and sometimes is accompanied by bleeding within the brain. Although most cases are mild, encephalitis can be severe and potentially fatal. Therefore, prompt medical attention is critical.

Cause: Viruses cause all of the several diseases known as encephalitis. Among the most dangerous types are the equine (EE-kwiyn) group, so called because the viruses infect horses as well as humans. Spread by mosquitoes, these include *Eastern equine encephalitis,* found in the eastern United States; *Western equine encephalitis,* found throughout the United States; and *Venezuelan equine encephalitis,* found in subtropical and tropical regions of the Americas. Other mosquito-spread infections include St. Louis, California, and West Nile encephalitis, named for the locations where they were first observed. In the United States the most common causes of encephalitis are viruses that are known as *enteroviruses*, cousins of poliomyelitis ("polio") that like polioviruses are shed in feces and commonly acquired when ingested.

In some cases encephalitis occurs as a secondary complication to other viral disorders, including measles, mumps, chicken pox, polio, herpes, and *Epstein-Barr infection* (mononucleosis). Newborn babies may develop encephalitis after being infected in the birth canal with genital herpesvirus.

Encephalitis also can result from drug reactions, chemotherapy, and poisoning, notably lead poisoning.

Noticeable symptoms: The first symptom is a persistent headache. A stiff neck, muscle aches, fever, fatigue or drowsiness, and nausea may develop. These physical symptoms are followed—anywhere from one to ten days later—by neurological problems such as confusion, personality changes, dementia, convulsions, and paralysis. In some cases there is coma (unconsciousness).

Diagnosis: If encephalitis is suspected, the doctor will probably remove a small amount of cerebrospinal fluid for analysis. An MRI (magnetic resonance imaging) scan or electroencephalogram (scan of brain waves) may be taken to confirm the diagnosis.

Treatment options: The patient requires rest in a darkened room and careful monitoring for changes in the brain. In most cases treatment is aimed mainly at controlling symptoms, such as headaches and fever, and maintaining the functions of the kidneys, lungs, and other vital organs. Steroids may be used to lower brain swelling. Antiviral drugs may be prescribed, especially for herpes-induced encephalitis.

Stages and progress: Encephalitis starts as a minor illness with few symptoms, but it can progress rapidly to coma and death. With prompt treatment most people recover completely even if very ill, although the illness may be fatal to infants and those over 65. Others may have permanent impairment, such as memory loss, hearing defects, or lack of muscle coordination. The outcome is determined mainly by the cause, the extent of brain inflammation, and the patient's general condition.

Endocarditis

(EHN-doh-kahr-DIY-tihs)

DISEASE

TYPE: INFECTIOUS
(BACTERIAL)

See also
Bacteria and disease
Blood poisoning
Congenital heart defects
Embolism
Heart
Heart murmur
Hemophilus influenzae **type B**
Mitral stenosis and incompetence
Prolapse of mitral valve
"Strep"

Phone doctor

Endocarditis is an infection of the endocardium (EHN-doh-KAHR-dee-um), the tissue that lines the inner walls of the heart and covers the heart valves.

Cause: Endocarditis occurs when bacteria, funguses, or other organisms attack the inner lining of the heart and the heart valves. The immune system walls off the infection, forming small wartlike bodies in heart tissue. These interfere with the operation of the valves and allow blood to leak through. Clots formed around bacterial bodies can be carried by the bloodstream to the brain, lungs, legs, or elsewhere, resulting in stroke or other serious disorders.

Organisms may enter the bloodstream during an operation or dental work. People who use dirty syringes or needles to inject drugs can easily become infected.

Incidence: Endocarditis is rare, especially in children and people over 60. It is most likely to affect drug users or people who have heart valve disease or an artificial valve.

Noticeable symptoms: Typical symptoms include a persistent low-grade fever or an unusually high fever. Either form may be accompanied by flulike symptoms—chills, fatigue, headache, loss of appetite, and aching joints. Often tiny red dots of broken blood vessels appear on the chest, back, fingers, or toes. There may be small lumps on the fingers or dark spots behind the fingernails caused by hemorrhaging. ***Call your physician if you have lengthy or high fevers or if you develop small hemorrhages under the nails or skin.*** Untreated endocarditis can be fatal.

If a blood clot from the damaged heart lodges in the brain, there also may be stroke symptoms, such as weakness or confusion. Similarly, leaky valves can produce symptoms of heart failure.

Diagnosis: Using a stethoscope, the physician may hear a slight fluttering sound, or heart murmur. This is a sign that blood is leaking through a damaged heart valve. From the images produced by an ultrasound scan or an echocardiogram (EHK-oh-KAHR-dee-uh-GRAAM) the physician can tell where heart valve damage has occurred and the seriousness of the damage. If endocarditis is detected, the physician will take blood samples to find out the kind of organism that is involved.

Treatment options: The patient will most likely be hospitalized. If bacteria are thought to be the cause of endocarditis, an antibiotic will be administered through a tube inserted in a vein in the arm. The patient continues taking an antibiotic for about a month after leaving the hospital. Then, for several months he or she will need to have frequent checkups to make sure the infection does not return. If there has been serious damage to a heart valve, surgical replacement of the valve may be necessary.

Prevention: Bacteria of the type commonly found in the mouth, where they are harmless, can cause endocarditis if they enter the bloodstream. This is most likely to happen to someone who has an existing heart murmur or other valve disorder. People who have damaged or artificial heart valves must generally take antibiotics before and after any dental work that might cause gum bleeding. Similar precautions are needed before and after other surgery.

Endocrine system

(EHN-duh-krihn)

BODY SYSTEM

Body organs whose only known role is to produce chemicals that regulate bodily functions are called *glands*. Many organs in the body, including the brain, heart, nerves, and small intestine, produce regulatory chemicals; but because these organs also have other functions, they usually are not called glands.

Traditionally the glands are treated as two separate systems—the endocrine and the exocrine—but there is some overlap between the two. *Endo-* means "inside," while *exo-* means "outside." The endocrine glands produce fluids that seep from the glands into the bloodstream; but tubes known as *ducts* carry secretions of the exocrine glands to their destinations. Endocrine glands are also called *ductless glands* because they rely on blood instead of ducts.

Role: Regulatory chemicals produced by endocrine glands are known as *hormones*. These determine such basic conditions as rate of metabolism, reproductive state, and chemical composition and pressure of blood. Furthermore, hormones control patterns and rates of growth in various parts of the body.

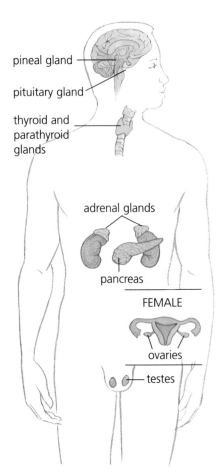

pineal gland

pituitary gland

thyroid and parathyroid glands

adrenal glands

pancreas

FEMALE

ovaries

testes

Endocrine glands and their functions

Adrenals	Help regulate blood pressure, blood sugar, and the sex drive; partially control metabolism
Ovaries	Produce hormones that regulate pregnancy; induce female secondary sexual characteristics; help control calcium uptake into bones
Pancreas	Controls blood sugar; as part of the digestive system, acts as an exocrine gland that releases chemicals that break down fats, carbohydrates, and proteins into the small intestine
Parathyroids	Regulate the release of stored calcium from bones
Pineal	Responds to light and helps regulate reproduction
Pituitary	"Master gland" under control of the brain; produces hormones that control many other glands; produces growth hormone
Testes	Produce sperm and secondary sexual characteristics in males
Thyroid	Regulates metabolism, growth, and calcium uptake by bones

Size and location: None of the endocrine glands are very large; most are the size of a walnut or smaller, although the pancreas is considerably larger. However, the part of the pancreas that is an endocrine gland consists of the tiny *islets of Langerhans,* which are scattered through the softball-sized gland. In each islet three different kinds of cells produce three different hormones. While insulin from the beta cells raises levels of glucose in the blood, the hormone glucagon from the alpha cells reduces blood glucose. The delta cells, a third islet cell group, produce a hormone that probably causes the small intestine to contract, although the function of the delta cells is not completely understood at this time.

Endocrine glands are located from the brain (pineal and pituitary) to just below the trunk (the testes), but most are in the trunk itself. In some cases the location of an endocrine gland seems to be significant. The pituitary is apparently lodged in the brain because many of its functions are directly controlled by brain structures. The pineal gland also needs to be located in the head, but for a different reason; it has to sense diffuse light.

Conditions that affect the endocrine system: Too little or too much of any one hormone can cause significant effects in almost all parts of the body. A prime example is diabetes mellitus, caused by too little insulin action. Most other diseases of this type are discussed in the entry Hormone disorders. Often the cause of changes in hormone production is a tumor, benign or cancerous, on an endocrine gland. In some cases, including diabetes mellitus type I, an autoimmune disorder affects the endocrines.

Endometriosis
(EHN-doh-mee-TREE-OH-SIHS)

DISEASE

TYPE: UNKNOWN

See also
Fallopian tubes
Menstrual pain
Reproductive system
Uterus

A woman's uterus is lined with a special type of tissue called the endometrium. In endometriosis this tissue grows outside its normal location in such places as the ovaries, fallopian tubes, peritoneum (PEHR-uh-tuh-NEE-uhm), and—in rare cases—sites outside the pelvic cavity, such as the lungs and underarms. When endometrial tissue grows in the walls of the uterus, the condition is called *adenomyosis* (AAD-n-oh-miy-OH-sihs)

Cause: The endometrium responds to hormones that are triggered during a woman's menstrual cycle. Each month it changes in thickness and complexity. If pregnancy does not occur, the endometrium breaks down, and menstrual flow begins. Misplaced endometrial tissue also responds to the hormones: Each month it bleeds, causing inflammation and scarring.

Incidence: An estimated 2.5 to 7.5% of women between the ages of puberty and menopause have endometriosis. Up to 50% of infertile women are believed to have the disorder; the infertility may be a result of endometriosis or be caused by the unknown mechanism that also produces endometriosis.

Noticeable symptoms: While some women with endometriosis are pain-free, others experience severe menstrual cramps, irregular menstrual periods, abdominal soreness, and pain during intercourse. In some cases infertility results. A woman with any of these symptoms should seek medical help.

Diagnosis: The doctor will conduct a pelvic examination. If endometriosis is suspected, laparoscopy (LAAP-uh-ROS-kuh-pee) will be performed in a hospital. In this procedure, performed under a general anesthetic, a slender instrument called a *laparo-scope* (LAAP-uhr-uh-SKOHP) is inserted into the pelvic cavity through a small cut in the navel. A light in the instrument enables the doctor to see scar tissue and other abnormalities.

Treatment options: There is no guaranteed cure for endometriosis. However, if detected early, the pain of endometriosis can usually be controlled with medication that reduces the amount of female hormones circulating in the blood. Drug treatment does not improve fertility.

If the condition is not diagnosed until it is advanced, treatment is more difficult. Surgery may be needed to remove some of the scar tissue; this may or may not improve fertility. A hysterectomy (HIHS-tuh-REHK-tuh-mee—removal of the uterus) or oophorectomy (OH-uh-fuh-REHK-tuh-mee—removal of the ovaries) may be performed, but only as a last resort. Even such drastic treatment is not effective for pain relief in all cases.

Symptoms disappear with menopause, however.

Prevention: Birth control methods that suppress menstruation often prevent endometriosis during the period they are used, but the disorder may reappear when use is stopped.

Environment and disease

REFERENCE

Many diseases are caused by substances in the environment rather than by bacteria, viruses, or genetics. People from ancient times suspected, often incorrectly but with a grain of truth, that some unknown effect of place or air causes illness. The fever thought to be caused by the air from marshes and swamps was called *mal aria* ("bad air"); the disorder is now known to be the mosquito-borne disease malaria.

Danger as the environment changes: The environment has changed since early times, often with serious effects on health. Some elements by themselves (for example, lead and cadmium) or in various compounds (for example, mercury) can produce disease in humans. In their natural state these elements are dispersed throughout rocks and soil. Thus, before mining and processing began, people encountered these poisons so seldom that the chemical elements posed little hazard. But today human activities have put concentrations of chemicals in exactly the same places as people.

Lead is a particular concern. High levels of lead cause symptoms of poisoning, but it has long been argued that even low levels of lead in children reduce intelligence. Later in life lead may cause similar damage in adults, particularly pregnant or lactating women and older adults with osteoporosis.

Even an innocuous element such as carbon can become a hazard. Coal, which is mainly carbon, becomes soot when burned. As early as the eighteenth century it was recognized that exposure to a great deal of soot resulted in cancer in chimney sweeps. Today soot from burning fossil fuels, including petroleum and coal, is a major worldwide health problem. In the United States calculations of the Environmental Protection Agency and the Harvard School of Public Health establish that exposure to airborne soot kills as many as 60,000 persons a year—mainly people with respiratory problems, including asthma, emphysema, and pneumonia.

A *carcinogen* (kahr-SIHN-uh-juhn) is a substance that causes cancer after repeated or prolonged exposure to it. After soot no carcinogens were recognized until well into the twentieth century, when it became evident that exposure to radioactive elements also induces cancer. By the 1950s there was clear-cut evidence that asbestos and tobacco smoke could be added to the list of carcinogens.

Radon is an elemental gas that seeps from certain rock formations as a by-product of the natural radioactivity of minerals in Earth's crust. In some places, such as mines or home basements, radon gas collects. In such situations humans breathe air laced with radon. Breathing radon-enriched air leaves behind radioactive particles that can cause cancer. This is well established for miners, although less certain in homes.

The list of modern hazards is a long one. Too much ozone, produced by automobile exhausts, damages lung tissue, while too little ozone in the stratosphere increases the risk of skin cancer from solar radiation. Fertilizer runoff from farming encourages dangerous algae to grow in ocean bays. Even infectious disease can be encouraged by environmental change; global warming attributed to human-produced carbon dioxide is spreading tropical diseases such as malaria into the former temperate zones.

Artificial chemical hazards: In the nineteenth century chemists began to produce synthetic versions of natural substances. Some artificial materials such as Teflon are nearly inert. More often, however, an organism *almost* recognizes an artificial chemical and tries to use it in place of a natural one that it resembles. For example, some synthetic chemicals may be recognized incorrectly by the body as the hormone estrogen, possibly promoting the growth of certain types of cancer.

Pesticides, used to kill insects, weeds, or fungi, are generally artificial and are designed to interfere with specific life processes. Although pesticides target processes in nonhuman creatures, all living things tend to use the same chemical pathways. As a result most pesticides can cause harm to humans when they are applied as general residues in the environment or in or on food that humans consume.

In the United States currently there are officially tolerated amounts of pesticide residue in foods sold in interstate commerce. The acceptable amounts are those found by the government to pose a reasonable certainty of causing no harm, but standards are stricter for foods normally consumed by young children.

Health hazards at work: In 1989 the U.S. Occupational Safety and Health Administration issued standards for 428 substances found in workplace air that could cause health hazards.

One of the earliest examples of a known workplace hazard was the recognition that workers' exposure to lead could lead to illness. In the sixteenth century Paracelsus pointed out that miners and smelters of metals developed a number of diseases from the vapors and dust of mining. A hundred years later Bernardino Ramazzini discussed how specific diseases were connected to specific occupations, noting that only the lowest class of doctors used mercury because better physicians knew that it could make the physicians themselves ill from repeated exposure.

Pesticides are a particular hazard to farm workers. In the

Precautions must be taken when dealing with fluids that release many molecules into the atmosphere at room temperatures. Such fluids, called *volatiles,* can produce lung damage or cancer.

Diseases of air pollution at work

Disease	Environmental causes	Symptoms
Asbestosis	Breathing air that contains asbestos fibers (made worse by tobacco smoking); common among asbestos miners, but also found in construction workers who use asbestos-based materials	Breathlessness; characteristic scars visible on x-rays; may be a precursor of lung cancer but is often fatal itself as shortness of breath gradually becomes inability to breathe at all
Black lung disease (anthracosis)	Breathing coal dust over a long period of time	Breathlessness and a cough that brings up black phlegm; black lumps develop in air passages, followed by emphysema
Brown lung disease	Breathing cotton dust regularly, usually at a textile mill	Breathlessness and cough
Pneumoconiosis	Breathing fine particles, including aluminum, beryllium, talc, sugar-cane, and synthetic fibers	Breathlessness and a cough that brings up phlegm or sputum
Siderosis	Breathing fine iron particles, usually in mining or some forms of machine work	While iron particles in the lungs produce the usual symptoms of pneumoconiosis, iron also leaches into the bloodstream, causing anemia, and then builds up in organs, interfering with normal function
Silicosis	Breathing rock particles	Breathlessness and cough; can lead to cancer

United States workers must be trained in the use of protective gear, given a place to clean up after exposure, and be provided with emergency care if needed. Workers are also barred from the fields for a specified amount of time after spraying. Despite such precautions, farm workers have higher death rates from disease than most other employment groups.

Prevention and risk reduction: Many environmental problems are attacked at a government level instead of at a personal level—air pollution, work safety, and pesticide residues require regulation. A person does have control over some forms of pollution, however. One can wear a nose-and-mouth filter when working in dusty environments, such as when sanding or installing insulation; adequate ventilation when using chemicals such as paint removers is essential; pesticides should be handled with care and residues washed from food; and so forth. Above all, do not use tobacco in any form.

Epidemics

The word *epidemic* means "commonly encountered in people," but the word casts fear into physicians and the general public, for in an epidemic the thing commonly encountered is disease and often death.

The first epidemic reported in detail was the "plague of Athens," caused not by the disease plague but by some fever that has not been definitely identified—possibilities range from mundane influenza to the exotic Rift Valley fever that sometimes occurs in parts of Africa. After the start of war between Sparta and Athens, when there was considerable travel and Athens was crowded with refugees, the powerful fever struck in 430 B.C. About one in three of those sickened died, while others lost fingers or limbs to gangrene caused by the "plague."

Among the infectious diseases that have ravaged whole continents and more are plague, syphilis, smallpox, yellow fever, cholera, influenza, polio, and AIDS. Today knowledge of how the diseases are transmitted has limited the number of people infected with plague or yellow fever; better treatment has made cholera less deadly; vaccination has slowed influenza, reduced polio cases to a trickle, and eliminated smallpox; but the rise of recent experiences with cholera and AIDS has shown that epidemics can still sweep through populations.

An epidemic may affect only one city or some small region. Scientists use the word *pandemic* ("all people") to describe epidemics that spread to large regions, whole continents, or around the world.

Pattern of an epidemic: Typically, an epidemic occurs when an infectious disease—especially one that is spread through the air, by animals, or by sexual transmission—reaches a population that has not been exposed to the disease previously. Individuals with no natural immunity are easily infected, and each one transmits the disease to many others. The number infected can double every few weeks. In the case of a disease spread by insects, the more humans that are infected, the more insects that can pick up the disease in a bite and transfer it.

Soon, however, the people who most easily can develop the disease have either gained immunity to it or have died from it. There are fewer and fewer sources of infection. Eventually, the disease reaches a low level and may even disappear from a population completely.

Sometimes natural immunity does not develop after infection. In that case many, or even most, individuals with the disease may continue transmitting the disease to others, either directly or by providing the disease to biting insects. There is no epidemic, but the disease may affect millions each year. In such instances the disease is said to be *endemic* ("dwelling in a place").

Plague: The main pandemic in historical times was of *bubonic plague*, which started in Asia in the thirteenth century and reached Europe in 1347. Plague is spread most often by fleas carried by rats (some forms of plague can also be spread directly from person to person, however). Estimates vary, but a common report is that the population of Europe was reduced by the disease to about two-thirds of its prepandemic size during the first waves and that the population did not fully recover until about 1450. Plague continued in several pandemic waves for another 250 years. Smaller epidemics occurred well into the twentieth century.

Syphilis: Most scholars today think that syphilis was present in all parts of the world from earliest times, but a modern epidemic in Europe began shortly after the voyages of Columbus, causing speculation that it was an American disease brought to the Old World by sailors. The beginning of the epidemic in 1495 started, like the plague of Athens, during war. For the next half century syphilis was epidemic, killing many and changing sexual practices as the method of transmission became better understood. As with most epidemics the worst ravages of the disease ended when the most susceptible individuals had been killed and a less virulent strain had replaced the lethal form.

Smallpox: Medical historians believe that the smallpox virus was spread originally by the expansion of the Arab state during the period between the seventh and tenth centuries. As an epidemic, however, smallpox came into its own when early adventurers accidentally brought the disease to a population that had never experienced it. A terrible epidemic of smallpox, abetted by other European infectious diseases, weakened or destroyed the Native American civilization. Whole villages, cities, and peoples were virtually wiped out.

Meanwhile, a strain of smallpox that was deadly to Europeans began to spread westward from Turkey. Starting in Venice about 1550 and spreading throughout Europe by 1700, smallpox killed about 60 million Europeans during the eighteenth century. At the end of that century, however, vaccination was developed, and soon smallpox was in retreat. By 1977 the last case naturally acquired was reported.

Yellow fever: Like bubonic plague, the terror of yellow fever was enhanced by a poor understanding of how it is transmitted. Not knowing that it is mosquito-borne, people could not understand the way the epidemic seemed to skip some people and take others, even within a single family. Yellow fever may have originated in Africa, but it reached more susceptible populations in the Americas and offshore islands starting in 1647. Epidemics of yellow fever raged from city to city throughout the Americas for the next 250 years. When the role of mosquitoes became understood, people were able to stop the disease's spread by taking strong measures to reduce mosquito populations.

Cholera: Cholera is an ancient terror that is thought to have originated in India, where it is endemic to this day. The nineteenth century saw several pandemics that covered much of the world. The first, from 1817 to 1825, spread from India throughout Asia and into Russia. The second wave started in India in 1826 and spread through Europe and into North America, halting around 1838. Two years later another pandemic began in India; that one lasted in parts of the world until 1873. During the wave from 1879 through 1883 Robert Koch identified and studied the bacterium that causes the disease, *Vibrio cholerae*. His studies were to aid in eventually halting the massive pandemics, although there were two more before World War II. In the 1990s tens of thousands were killed by a cholera epidemic in South America and another among refugees from wars in Africa.

Influenza: It is not surprising that World War I produced its own pandemic. War, especially on a large scale, provides a perfect setting for disease—large populations huddled together, rapid travel from place to place, shortages of food that weaken immune defenses, and wounded populations that are even weaker than the starving. Influenza is a disease that occurs in pandemics on a regular basis whenever a new strain develops in its homeland of eastern Asia. The influenza pandemic of 1917–1918 was notable because the strain of the disease was especially deadly, killing the young and healthy as well as the infirm and old. Millions of people around the world died.

AIDS: The example of AIDS (acquired immunodeficiency syndrome), a syndrome caused by infection with the human immunodeficiency virus (HIV), shows that a modern pandemic can occur with the full force of the great epidemics of the past. Although the spread of HIV infection in the United States has been kept to tens of thousands of new cases each year, worldwide the epidemic infects nearly 50 million persons annually. Nearly all of those infected eventually die from complications due to the disease, although death is often a matter of years after infection instead of days as in most other epidemic diseases.

Scientists did not know what caused AIDS or how it spread when the pandemic started. They still do not have a vaccine that prevents the disease, but knowledge of how the disease is transmitted makes it possible for an individual to be safe from it. Despite this knowledge, lack of education or simple carelessness has already made AIDS the fourth leading cause of death worldwide.

Epiglottitis

See **Hemophilus influenzae type B**

Epilepsy

DISORDER

TYPE: UNKNOWN OR GENETIC

Epilepsy has been well known since ancient times. Its name comes from a Greek word for "seizure." Seizures are sudden changes in brain function that cause loss of consciousness, involuntary movements, or abnormal sensory experiences, often in combination.

Seizures result from abnormal bursts of activity in the nerve cells (*neurons*) of the *cerebral cortex*. This is the outer layer of the brain that controls consciousness, sensory awareness, voluntary movement, and thought.

Seizures themselves are quite common. Many people experience them at least once during their lives. But those that occur just once, or only a few times within a brief period, are not considered epilepsy. Epilepsy is characterized by repeated seizures, often beginning in childhood and persisting anywhere from a few years to a lifetime.

There are two basic forms of epilepsy. The *generalized* form affects the whole cortex; the *partial* form affects only a limited area. Generalized epilepsy in turn has two main manifestations: *tonic clonic seizures* (*grand mal*) and *absence seizures* (*petit mal* [PEHT-ee mahl]). Partial epilepsy also has two principal manifestations: *simple* and *complex*.

Tonic clonic seizures often begin with an abrupt, hoarse cry, accompanied by the loss of consciousness and muscle control, so that the individual falls insensible to the ground. The body goes into a tonic convulsion—muscles throughout the body suddenly contract, causing overall rigidity.

For another minute or two the convulsions become clonic—rhythmical muscle contractions that cause jerking, twitching, or shuddering. A period of deep sleep, lasting several minutes to half an hour, usually follows. Upon awaking, the individual has no memory of the experience.

Absence seizures start with a brief, vacant stare, followed by blinking and a loss of consciousness, all lasting for no more than 30 seconds. There is no loss of muscle tone, and the individual has no memory of the experience.

Simple partial seizures cause clonic jerking or twitching that usually begins in a single part of the body, such as an arm or leg or part of the face. They may be confined to that area or may spread to one or more other areas. There is no loss of consciousness or memory, but the individual may experience abnormal sensations (of taste, smell, sight, sound, or touch), may feel nauseated, or may be swept by baseless fear or anger.

Complex partial seizures produce effects similar to those of simple partial seizures, except that the affected individual enters a trancelike state, disconnected from normal consciousness. The individual appears dazed and confused and cannot interact normally with others. Actions may be uncontrolled and repetitive. On recovery the individual will probably not recall anything of the attack.

Cause: In seven out of ten cases the cause of epilepsy cannot be precisely identified. There is a slight tendency to run in families, so some instances may be of genetic origin. Epilepsy is also a common component of other genetic conditions such as Down syndrome. Some instances, especially those that occur in later life, can be traced to brain damage, either from disease or injury.

Epilepsy often occurs as one manifestation of other central nervous system disorders, particularly cerebral palsy and developmental disability (mental retardation).

Incidence: Epilepsy is the most common central nervous system disorder after developmental disability. It afflicts about 2.3 million Americans of all ages. Half of these are diagnosed before they are 25 years old, but almost a quarter of occurrences begin in persons over 65.

Noticeable symptoms: Absence seizures may be mistaken for daydreaming, and simple partial seizures may pass unnoticed by others. But tonic clonic and complex partial seizures have quite evident and distinctive manifestations.

Diagnosis: Diagnosis mainly depends on medical history, reinforced by *electroencephalography* (EEG [ih-LEHK-troh-ehn-SEHF-uh-LAHG-ruh-fee]), which measures brain activity in terms of the oscillating electrical charges (brain waves) it produces. Each type of epilepsy produces its own distinctive kind of abnormal waves.

Treatment options: Most epilepsy can be treated successfully with *anticonvulsant drugs,* which either eliminate seizures entirely or at least control them satisfactorily. For the minority of individuals whose epilepsy is not relieved by drugs alone, other forms of treatment can be employed.

Children may be put on a special *ketogenic* (KEE-toh-JEHN-ihk) diet, which is high in fats and low in protein and carbohydrates. It causes the body to burn fat rather than glucose (sugar) for energy, and as a side effect tends to reduce the frequency and severity of seizures.

Many individuals find it possible to control seizures with *vagus nerve stimulation.* A small battery implanted under the skin supplies periodic pulses of electricity to the vagus nerve extending from the neck into the brain.

If the part of the brain where the seizures originate can be precisely located, it may be possible to remove that segment surgically without damaging normal brain function. Surgery, however, is generally a treatment of last resort.

Outlook: For the majority of those affected, the long-term outlook is good. With treatment almost 60% achieve lasting remission from seizures within a year or two after being diagnosed. Another 15% achieve remission over a longer period. About one in four, however, continues to experience seizures indefinitely, although treatment may help reduce their frequency.

Epileptic seizures ordinarily last only a short time and cause no lasting physical harm. The exception—uncommon but not rare—is a condition called *status epilepticus,* in which seizures are long-lasting (over 30 minutes) and severe to the point of being life-threatening. The principal danger of epilepsy, however, is of accidents during seizures.

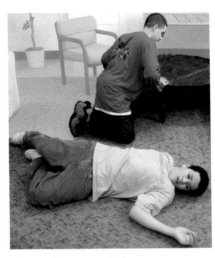

The main way to help a person experiencing an epileptic seizure is to make sure he or she can rest comfortably, and to move away any furniture or other objects that might cause harm. It is not advisable to put anything in the mouth to prevent biting.

Esophagus

(ih-SOF-uh-guhs)

BODY SYSTEM

Also known as the *gullet,* the esophagus is the muscular tube through which food moves on its way from the mouth to the stomach. Its opening to the stomach has a valve called the *lower esophageal* (ih-SOF-uh-JEE-uhl) *sphincter* at its base to prevent food from traveling back up again.

Size and location: The esophagus is nine or ten inches long and less than an inch in diameter. It is one of the passageways through the diaphragm, going between the lungs above the diaphragm and then meeting the stomach just below the diaphragm.

Role: The esophagus consists of rings of muscles that contract and expand in relation to the position of food in the passage. The presence of a bite of food causes the ring of muscle above the food to shrink, while the part of the tube where food is located grows wider. This moves the bite downward and evokes a wave that carries the bite down the tube, through the diaphragm, and into the stomach. Meanwhile the muscles above relax and wait for the next bite.

Conditions that affect the esophagus: A pain felt in the middle of the upper part of the chest is called heartburn, but a more appropriate name would be esophagus burn, since heartburn is caused by stomach acid attacking the walls of the lower part of the esophagus. Persistent heartburn, or GERD (gastroesophageal reflux disease), is caused by failure of the lower esophageal sphincter. Less often, it may be a symptom of a hernia at the point where the esophagus joins the stomach. GERD is often a consequence of obesity or of alcohol abuse. In some individuals GERD leads to changes in the lower esophagus termed *Barrett's esophagus,* a precursor of cancer.

Difficulty in swallowing is a symptom of almost all esophageal problems other than heartburn. Since such a difficulty is a major symptom of cancer of the esophagus, ***consult your physician anytime you experience persistent difficulty in swallowing.*** One form, *neurogenic dysphasia* (dihs-FAY-zhuh), may be a symptom of diseases that affect the central nervous system, such as Parkinson's or Alzheimer's disease; or it may be a symptom of other diseases of the nerves, such as multiple sclerosis or ALS (amyotrophic lateral sclerosis).

Achalasia (AAK-uh-LAY-zhuh) also causes swallowing difficulty along with other symptoms. The problem is that the lower esophageal sphincter stays closed, leaving food in the esophagus. The condition can be relieved with mechanical dilation or with surgery or other means to relax the muscles that keep the lower esophageal sphincter closed.

Bleeding varices (VEHR-ih-seez) are varicose veins in the esophagus caused by damage to the liver, nearly always in response to alcoholism. This condition can be fatal but usually goes away completely when the alcoholic stops drinking.

Yeasts and viruses can infect the esophagus, leading to esophagitis caused by *Candida,* herpes, or cytomegalovirus.. Swallowed chemicals can damage the walls of the esophagus, including pills that get stuck there. Vomiting can also damage the esophagus.

Phone doctor

See also

Alcoholism

ALS (amyotrophic lateral sclerosis)

Alzheimer's disease

Bulimia

Cancers

Candidiasis

Cirrhosis of the liver

Cold sore

Congenital digestive system conditions

Digestive system

GERD (gastroesophageal reflux disease)

Guillain-Barré syndrome

Heartburn

Hernias

Huntington's disease

Multiple sclerosis

Myasthenia gravis

Obesity

Scleroderma

Sore throat

Veins

Excretory system

(EHK-skrih-TAWR-ee)

BODY SYSTEM

Excretory system

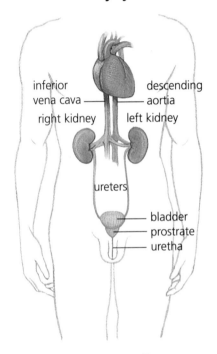

inferior
vena cava
right kidney

descending
aortia
left kidney

ureters

bladder
prostrate
uretha

The excretory system collects wastes from the blood that can be dissolved in water and also insoluble wastes converted to tiny particles. The combination, known as urine, is then expelled from the body.

As the body functions, it continually produces wastes that are liquids, solids, and gases. These wastes are removed in various ways, but the name excretory system refers exclusively to the principal system that collects and removes liquid waste. Although considerable water is excreted along with gases during respiration, and various exocrine glands also excrete minor amounts of liquid waste (notably sweat and tears), removal of these liquid wastes is usually not considered part of the excretory system.

Size and location: The excretory system of liquid waste is normally considered to be the two kidneys, two tubes called *ureters* (yoo-REE-tuhrz) that connect the kidneys to a storage sac called the *bladder,* and a tube from the bladder to the exterior of the body called the *urethra* (yoo-REE-thruh). All are located in the middle and lower abdomen (in males the urethra extends through the penis).

The liver processes chemical waste for removal but is not considered part of the excretory system. The prostate gland in males is directly on the urethra; although not a part of the excretory system, the prostate can affect excretion of urine adversely if it becomes enlarged.

Role: Waste products from energy production or from reshaping cells or tissues continuously enter the bloodstream. Water is one of those wastes, since the "ash" of burning fats or carbohydrates for energy is entirely water and carbon dioxide. While the lungs handle carbon dioxide, nearly all water must be removed by the kidneys. The kidneys also remove other wastes that are carried in water. The combination of water and other wastes is called *urine.* It normally consists of 19 parts water to 1 part other material.

- Protein destruction produces not only water and carbon dioxide but also nitrogen compounds. The liver converts the nitrogen compounds into urea, which is removed from the blood by the kidneys and dissolved in water.
- The chemicals RNA and DNA break down as well; they are converted to uric acid, which also becomes part of urine.

■ Waste products that cannot be dissolved in water are processed into tiny solid particles that float in urine the way that small particles of soil float in muddy water.

Conditions that affect the excretory system: Because the body produces different wastes when it is not functioning properly, chemical analysis of urine is an important diagnostic tool. Kidney or bladder diseases and kidney or bladder stones are breakdowns of the excretory system. If urine production is halted completely by a kidney breakdown, death from waste accumulation occurs quickly. If a swollen prostate keeps urine from being excreted, severe illness results. When more uric acid is produced than the kidneys remove, crystals lodged in joints become painful gout. Both the kidneys and the bladder are sites of moderately rare cancers.

Diseases that cause too much urine to be produced are the various forms of diabetes, none of which has its origin in the excretory system, however. Loss of control of the waste-removal system is incontinence.

Bladder infections, also known as *cystitis,* are common but usually not dangerous.

Exocrine glands

(EHK-suh-KRIHN)

BODY SYSTEM

There are two main types of glands, known as exocrine and endocrine. Glands with ducts—tubes that carry fluids from the glands to a specific location—are called exocrine. Glands whose fluids seep directly into the blood are called endocrine.

In principle, any organ that produces and releases (*secretes*) a fluid is called a gland. However, many organs in the body, including the brain, heart, nerves, and small intestine, secrete fluids but also have other functions; these are usually not called glands. The liver is a borderline case, often considered a gland although its other functions may be more important.

The word "gland" comes from "acorn" in Latin; it originally denoted the *lymph nodes.* When disease causes lymph

Principal exocrine glands

Apocrine	Large glands that release sweat mixed with a smelly fluid; found under the arms, near the organs of reproduction, near the breasts, and near the anus, these glands are thought to help stimulate sexual responses.
Kidneys	The fluid that the kidneys release is called *urine,* one of the main waste products of vertebrate animals, including humans.
Liver	As an exocrine gland the liver produces *bile,* a mixture of powerful chemicals that are carried to the intestines either directly or after storage in the gallbladder; in the intestines bile helps break down fats; it has many other functions related to blood chemistry as well as its exocrine role.
Mammary	In females who have recently given birth, the mammary glands produce human milk, used to feed infants until they are ready for solid food; human milk also contains antibodies that aid an infant's immune system.
Mucous	Single-cell glands that line the digestive and respiratory systems, producing a protective lubricating fluid called *mucus;* the mucous glands are also known as *goblet cells* from their shape.
Oil glands	Glands in the skin at the base of hairs release lubricant needed to keep the skin supple and to help protect against germs; these are known as oil glands or as *sebaceous glands.*
Pancreas	As an exocrine gland the pancreas releases chemicals that break down fats, carbohydrates, and proteins in the small intestine, where the fluid known as *pancreatic juice* is carried.
Prostate	The prostate, located in men near the rectum, produces the fluid in which sperm swim, the main liquid component of *semen.*
Salivary	Glands near the mouth secrete a fluid that aids food in starting through the digestive system and that begins the process of breaking down large starch molecules into smaller molecules called sugars.
Sweat	Sweat glands, also called *eccrine glands,* help regulate temperature by releasing a salty fluid onto the surface of the skin.
Tear	Tear glands, also known as *lachrymal glands,* produce a salty fluid similar to sweat that helps lubricate and protect eyes, in part by carrying foreign bodies out of the eyes; the fluid is produced in greater amounts during strong emotions.
Wax	Glands in the ears secrete earwax.

nodes to be sore and enlarged, the old names continues to be used, and we speak of the sympton as "swollen glands."

Conditions associated with exocrine disorders: Diseases caused by malfunctioning exocrine glands range from life-threatening kidney failure to embarrassing blackheads caused by clogged oil glands. Perhaps the most general disease of the exocrine glands is cystic fibrosis, which affects both the mucous glands and the sweat glands. Failure to produce tears leads to eye disease, and overproduction of earwax can cause partial deafness. Disorders of the liver or pancreas interfere with digestion, often affecting the excretory system as well.

Eyes and vision

The eyes are the pair of organs concerned specifically with sight and the faculty of vision. Each eye consists of a nearly spherical structure about one inch in diameter located in a bony socket at the front of the skull. The exposed part of the eyeball includes, from front to back, the cornea, a transparent covering; the aqueous humor, a cushion of watery fluid; the iris and pupil, an expanding and contracting colored disc surrounding the black center through which light passes; and the lens, the focusing device that changes shape constantly. Behind this front part is the vitreous humor, a jellylike material that fills the eyeball and helps give the eyeball its round shape, and the retina, a mass of receptors known as *rods* and *cones* spread over the curved back wall of the eyeball. The receptors respond to tones of gray (rods) and to colors (cones) and convert the data to electrical impulses. From the retina the impulses travel through the optic nerve to a region of the brain specialized to receive and make sense of the signal.

Other critical parts of each eye consist of six muscles that control its movement; protective eyelids; the conjunctiva, a transparent membrane that covers the parts of the front of the eye not covered by the cornea and also the inner surface of the eyelids; and a tear (lachrymal [LAAK-ruh-muhl]) gland, whose moisture further protects the delicate surfaces of the eye.

Amblyopia (AAM-blee-OH-pee-uh): *Lazy eye,* as amblyopia is commonly called, is a condition in which one eye gradually ceases to function. Amblyopia typically occurs when the "lazy" eye has a refractive defect such as severe nearsightedness, misalignment (crossed eyes), or an astigmatism that remains untreated for several years. The different messages sent to the brain by the unmatched eyes are in conflict; to resolve the differences, the brain suppresses the poorer visual messages in favor of the better ones. The favored eye grows stronger and the one less used grows weaker, its nerve connections to the brain gradually ceasing to function.

Amblyopia is avoidable if the tendency toward it is corrected before the age of seven or eight. Using a patch to cover the better-seeing eye can retrain a deviated eye muscle. Glasses that take care of a refractive error are another common treat-

The eye is an intricate extension of the brain that in humans becomes the instrument of the most important sense, sight.

A "long" eyeball means that the focus is only on the retina when the object being seen is near—hence, nearsightedness.

A "short" eyeball similarly causes farsightedness. Presbyopia is farsightedness caused by eyes that are stiff and unable to focus well.

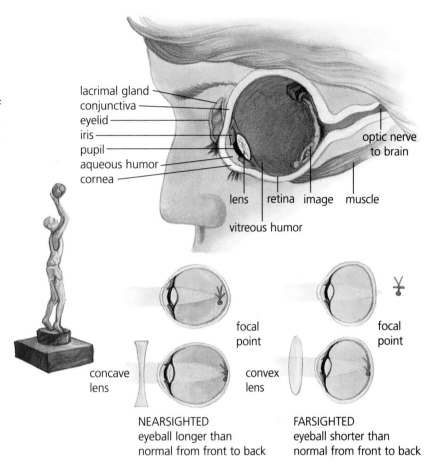

lacrimal gland
conjunctiva
eyelid
iris
pupil
aqueous humor
cornea

optic nerve to brain

lens | retina | image | muscle

vitreous humor

focal point

focal point

concave lens

convex lens

NEARSIGHTED
eyeball longer than normal from front to back

FARSIGHTED
eyeball shorter than normal from front to back

ment. Corrections that are delayed until after the neural connections to the young brain are formed are of little or no use.

Astigmatism (uh-STIHG-muh-TIHZ-uhm)**:** Astigmatism is a common condition caused by irregularities in the curvature of the cornea, the transparent front part of the eye. Since the astigmatic corneal surface is not symmetrical, horizontal focusing differs from vertical focusing. Corrective lenses made to compensate for specific irregularities solve the problem in most instances. Laser surgery has also been used to correct astigmatism in adults.

Color blindness: There are several forms of color blindness.
Most people with color blindness cannot distinguish reds from greens. This form of color blindness is a genetic defect found in

perhaps 8% of white males of European descent and smaller percentages of other groups. This inherited disorder is usually sex-linked—the majority of individuals affected are male. Women who have a single copy of this gene have normal vision, but may pass it on to their male children, who will then be color blind.

People who have trouble distinguishing between colors other than red or green may simply have a lower level of color perception, often caused by other eye diseases or simply by aging. Typically blue and green can be confused, especially if the colors are alike in brightness but not in hue.

Much more rare is *total color blindness,* loss of all color, yielding a world that appears in shades of black, gray, and white.

Double vision: *Diplopia* (dih-PLOH-pee-uh), popularly known as double vision, has several causes, the most common being defective eye muscles that fail to turn and focus the two eyes as a single unit. Young children, whose eye muscles are still developing, are particularly prone to diplopia, as the occasional case of crossed eyes and wall eye demonstrates. Diplopia may also occur as a temporary condition following a brain concussion or as the result of cataracts. In rare circumstances double vision may be a symptom of some other, more serious condition that coincidentally interferes with the normal functioning of the eyes.

Exophthalmos (EHK-suhf-THAAL-muhs): Exophthalmos is the medical term for *bulging eyes,* caused by swelling of soft tissue lining the eye socket. Exophthalmos most commonly results from thyroid disease, in which case both eyes are affected; or it may be a symptom of an eye tumor or an aneurysm, in which case only one eye may protrude. Vision may be distorted as a result, and treatment of both the symptom and the underlying cause is always indicated.

Keratoconjunctivitis (KEHR-uh-toh-kuhn-JUNGK-tuh-VIY-tihs): *Dry eye,* or keratoconjunctivitis, describes persistent drying of the outer surface of the eyeball caused by insufficient production of tears. The eyes feel gritty and irritated and may also be overly sensitive to light. Over time keratoconjunctivitis can result in thickening of the cornea and conjunctiva and damage to vision.

Often dry eye results from polluted air, but it may also be a secondary symptom of one of the autoimmune disorders, such as rheumatoid arthritis or "lupus" (systemic lupus erythematosus). The autoimmune attack on tissues in such diseases can damage the tear-producing glands.

Xerophthalmia (ZIR-uhf-THAAL-mee-uh) is a related disorder traceable to a deficiency of vitamin A. It has the potential to cause severe scarring of the cornea if not treated promptly. Xerophthalmia is largely restricted to populations whose diet is extremely poor. But the disorder can also occur in persons who have a faulty digestive system that is unable to absorb enough vitamin A despite a normal diet.

Dry eye caused by pollution may be relieved with frequent applications of artificial tears, which are sold in liquid form over the counter (no prescription needed) at pharmacies. If the condition persists, a physician should be consulted.

Nearsightedness and farsightedness: Nearsightedness is also called *myopia* (miy-OH-pee-uh), while farsightedness may be either *hyperopia* (HIY-puh-ROH-pee-uh) or *presbyopia* (PREHZ-bee-OH-pee-uh). Both conditions are refractive errors, or errors in focusing.

In nearsightedness the eyeball is abnormally long from front to back, causing difficulties in focusing on objects more than a foot or more distant. Nearsightedness often reveals itself early and can increase as children—and the eyeballs—grow. By age 21 about 35% of all Americans are myopic to some degree.

In farsightedness the eyeball is shorter than normal from front to back, causing difficulty in seeing nearby objects in sharp focus. Younger eyes can often accommodate to the abnormality by using the tiny ciliary muscles in the eye to increase the curvature of the lens as needed. Consequently, a lifelong condition of hyperopia may not be noticed until the individual reaches maturity, and accommodation is less successful. Approximately 60% of Americans are farsighted to some extent.

Presbyopia shares many visual similarities with hyperopia, but it is the farsightedness that is particular to older people, including those whose eyeballs are of normal dimension. In presbyopia the power of the eyes to focus on nearby objects weakens progressively, usually beginning around age 45, when reading small print becomes difficult. Almost everyone develops presbyopia in later years.

All three refractive errors are readily corrected with glasses or contact lenses. Laser surgery is a relatively new procedure that is being used for myopia, but it is only suitable for adults whose physical growth is over.

Night blindness: Night blindness can happen in people who have normal vision in daylight and other well-lighted situations. It results in difficulty driving at night and seeing in poorly lighted rooms. This may be an early symptom of vitamin A deficiency, cataracts, retinosa pigmentosa, or other medical problems. Night blindness is treated by correcting the underlying problem.

Nystagmus (nih-STAAG-muhs)**:** This is a condition in which the eyes move involuntarily, in a jerky horizontal, vertical, or circular motion. The disorder is almost always present at birth and is of unknown cause. Though the anatomy of the eyes may be normal, vision is usually affected to some degree. Some people with nystagmus are legally blind, while others lead full, normal lives. Nystagmus that appears in later life may be an indicator of a nervous disease or brain tumor.

Ptosis (TOH-sihs)**:** Ptosis is a drooping of the upper eyelid, usually due to a weakness of the lid-lifting muscle or interference with the nerve that operates the muscle. When it appears in children, it should be surgically corrected to prevent interference with sight. Acquired ptosis may be a sign of a neurological disease, such as myasthenia gravis, and should be brought to the attention of a physician.

Ectropion (ehk-TROH-pee-on) and *entropion* (ehn-TROH-pee-on) are other conditions that involve the eyelids, typically of older people. The former is a turning outward of the lid so as to expose the inner pink surface, usually in the lower lid of persons who have some sort of facial paralysis. Entropion is a turning inward of the lid, caused most often by growth of the lashes inward. Since eyelashes have the potential to scar the eye, surgical correction may be necessary if the condition persists.

Diseases that sometimes affect the eye: The skin disease rosacea may occur on the eyelids, producing itching and sometimes a burning sensation. Herpesviruses, most commonly cold sore viruses but sometimes the chicken pox virus, can infect the cornea and sometimes penetrate deeper into the eye. Both bacteria and fungi can invade the interior of the eyeball if they are given an opening through accident or surgery, producing an inflammation termed *endophthalmitis* (EHND-of-thuhl-MIY-tihs). Bacteria and fungi also can infect the region behind the eyeball, producing a dangerous and fast developing condition called *orbital cellulitis*. ***This condition, characterized by painful eye movement, double vision, and bulging eyes with swollen lids, must be treated immediately. Go to the emergency room of a hospital.*** Multiple sclerosis can inflame the optic nerve. Autoimmune diseases, such as rheumatoid arthritis, can damage the sclera, or white of the eye.

Emergency Room

Fainting

See **Dizziness**

Fallopian tubes

(fuh-LOH-pee-uhn)

BODY SYSTEM

The fallopian tubes, named for a sixteenth-century Italian anatomist, Gabriello Fallopio, are a pair of passages that link the uterus to the ovaries. Eggs (*ova*) travel through these tubes from an ovary to the uterus. During reproduction sperm deposited in the vagina also move through the tubes. If an egg is present in a tube, the sperm may meet and fertilize it, after which the fertilized egg continues through the tube to the uterus.

Size and location: Each tube is about 5 or 6 inches long. The end near the ovary widens and faces the ovary with a fringed opening. The fringes wave continuously toward the ovary. When an ovary releases a partially developed egg, the egg becomes caught in the fringes and directed into the fallopian tube, which carries the egg toward the uterus with sweeping motions of hairlike projections that line the tube.

Role: The egg continues its development as it travels through the tube. Sperm, if present, fertilize the developed egg. Hormones that were produced when the egg was released from the ovary prepare the uterus to receive a fertilized egg, which lodges itself in the wall of the uterus and begins to divide. If not fertilized, the egg, after a day or two in the tube, dies and disintegrates.

Phone doctor

Conditions that affect the fallopian tubes: A fertilized egg may fail to leave a tube, causing an ectopic pregnancy ("tubal pregnancy"). *A woman of childbearing age who develops abdominal pain lasting for more than a few hours should contact a physician.* Ectopic pregnancy can cause severe bleeding and lead to life-threatening shock.

Infection of the female reproductive system, called PID (pelvic inflammatory disease), generally includes the fallopian tubes along with other organs. Inflammation of the tubes, caused by infection, is called salpingitis (SAAL-pihn-JIY-tihs). Gonorrhea and chlamydia are common sexually transmitted diseases that may infect the tubes.

Both PID and gonorrhea may result in an abscess in a tube that could cause scarring that blocks the tube, making that tube no longer useful in reproduction. Often that tube must be removed surgically to eliminate the abscess, but reproduction requires only one working fallopian tube. If both fallopian tubes are inoperative, reproduction becomes impossible. Blocked fallopian tubes are a leading cause of infertility. Another possible cause of infertility or of pain is endometriosis, growth of tissue from the lining of the uterus in another location, such as within a fallopian tube.

Familial hypercholesterolemia

(HIY-puhr-kuh-LEHS-tuhr-uh-LEE-mee-uh)

DISEASE

TYPE: GENETIC

Atherosclerosis, a clogging of the arteries with fatty deposits, leads to many heart attacks and strokes each year. It is closely linked with a high level of cholesterol in the blood and is often considered to be associated with a diet rich in fat, made worse by lack of exercise. But many people also have a genetic disorder that causes excessive cholesterol in the blood, known as familial hypercholesterolemia, or FH.

Cause: Atherosclerosis is thought to be caused by an excess of "bad" cholesterol, known formally as *low-density lipoprotein*, or LDL. Cholesterol is produced by the liver, and when it reaches a certain level in the blood, the liver reabsorbs it and converts it to other substances. People with FH have defects in their liver cells that prevent the liver from absorbing LDL for conversion and also stimulate the production of even more LDL.

Incidence: FH is a dominant genetic disorder. Each child of an affected parent has a one-in-two chance of inheriting the defect. It appears in about one in five hundred births.

Noticeable symptoms: A family history of early heart disease may be evidence of FH. Affected individuals may have a yellowish circle around the iris of each eye or yellowish cholesterol deposits, called xanthomata, in the skin, especially around the eyes or on tendons.

Diagnosis: The level of LDL in the blood is persistently high, despite efforts to control it with diet and exercise. There are other conditions that produce similar high cholesterol levels, including low thyroid hormones and some kidney diseases. Some inherited triglyceride disorders also raise LDL levels. The physician will check levels of various blood components before reaching a final diagnosis.

Treatment options: Lifestyle changes such as a low-fat diet and regular exercise can bring LDL down to safe levels for many people. But for people with FH these methods usually must be combined with medications. The three most commonly prescribed are bile acid sequestrants such as cholestyramine, "statins" such as lovastatin, and niacin (vitamin B_3). The statins have become the drugs of choice for most people, although they may require regular monitoring of liver function since some patients develop liver damage from their use. Some evidence suggests that statins are beneficial beyond their role in lowering total and LDL cholesterol.

Most people with FH have a good chance for a normal life span if their condition is diagnosed early and treated carefully. Those that inherit the gene for FH from both parents are at high risk of early death from heart disease or stroke and require aggressive treatment, sometimes including liver transplant.

Farsightedness

See **Eyes and Vision**

Fatigue

SYMPTOM

Fatigue can stem from extended use of either the body or the brain in tasks that require long hours of labor or concentration. Whole-body and mental fatigue are also normal immune-system reactions to certain diseases, especially virus infections. Fatigue is truly nature's way of telling you to slow down, to gather your strength to fight the disease. Fatigue may also be localized as weakness and pain in skeletal muscles, especially the limbs or back, after heavy use.

Rest or sleep ordinarily relieves either the fatigued body or the sore muscle. In some illnesses, however, fatigue persists day after day despite efforts at sleep and renewal. In such cases fatigue may be caused by a serious underlying condition.

Cause: Muscle fatigue sets in when oxygen supplies are exhausted at the site of muscle cells, and muscle begins to use other resources for energy. The chemical changes that produce energy in this situation have lactic acid as a waste product. The nerves sense lactic acid and begin to signal fatigue. If the muscle continues in use, the lactic acid buildup eventually slows down muscle contraction; as a result one is forced to stop using the muscle. At this point fatigue becomes exhaustion.

Another common cause of whole-body fatigue is a low count of circulating red blood cells, or anemia. This condition produces fatigue partly because the red blood cells are the agents that carry oxygen to muscles. When less oxygen reaches muscles, they convert to lactic acid-producing chemical reactions sooner. Hepatitis and other liver diseases may cause

Rest

Practice meditation

fatigue through anemia, but these diseases also permit the buildup of toxic chemicals in the blood. Cancers of the blood cells or lymph system, such as leukemias and lymphomas, also have fatigue as a major symptom. Disorders of metabolism or calcium balance caused by poorly functioning thyroid, parathyroid, or pituitary glands produce fatigue as well. Another source of fatigue can be such medical treatments as radiation therapy for cancers.

Some parasites, notably tapeworm, produce fatigue by draining energy from the body. Not getting enough sleep also leads to fatigue. One physical cause for loss of sleep is apnea, temporary stoppage of breath during sleep.

Parts affected: Muscle fatigue can spread to whole-body tiredness as the lactic acid diffuses through the body. The causes of mental fatigue are uncertain but probably also involve wastes in the brain that build up faster than they are removed.

Related symptoms: A person experiencing fatigue has greatly reduced strength, finds it hard to concentrate, reacts slowly, and feels irritated, impatient, and depressed. A fatigued muscle aches sharply or knots in an acutely aching cramp.

Associations: Aside from overuse of muscles or lack of sleep, the most common cause of fatigue is minor viral illness. Immune-system reactions to infection include production of virus-fighting chemicals called *interferons* (IHN-tuhr-FEER-onz). Side effects of interferons include fever and fatigue. Such side effects also occur when interferons are used to fight diseases such as hepatitis C or multiple sclerosis.

Fatigue lasting over long periods of time for no obvious reason indicates the presence of an illness that should be treated. Serious illnesses with fatigue as one symptom include anemia, cystic fibrosis, diabetes, hepatitis, tuberculosis, clinical depression, and cancer. One form of long-lasting disease is known simply as chronic fatigue syndrome, since debilitating tiredness not relieved by rest or sleep is the main symptom.

Relief of symptoms: Rest and especially sleep, restraint of physical exertion, and reduction of mental stress—meditation

Phone doctor

often helps—are the most important steps to take to relieve fatigue. When these fail, fatigue may have a deeper cause. ***See a physician for fatigue that lasts days or weeks and is not relieved by rest.***

Prevention and possible actions: Muscle fatigue can be reduced with regular exercise. Muscles react to repeated use by gradually becoming bigger and increasing the blood flow, so that after a steady program of exercises muscles can work longer and harder before having to switch to oxygen-free energy production.

Fetal alcohol syndrome

DISORDER

TYPE: DEVELOPMENTAL

Women who drink heavily during pregnancy—particularly early pregnancy—run a high risk of bearing a child with a group of defects known as fetal alcohol syndrome. Some of these defects are physical malformations that originate during the early weeks of prenatal development, such as a small skull, small eye openings, and congenital heart defects. Malformations are usually accompanied by retarded growth and developmental disability (mental retardation), which can originate at any time during pregnancy.

There is a growing body of evidence that even moderate drinking during pregnancy can cause behavioral problems, such as ADHD (attention-deficit/hyperactivity disorder) and learning difficulties, in children.

Cause: Alcohol in a woman's blood easily passes through the placenta and umbilical cord to the fetus. There it breaks down less rapidly than it does in the mother's body and causes lasting damage.

Incidence: Between 2,000 and 12,000 babies are born with fetal alcohol syndrome in the United States each year. About ten times as many babies are born with at least some adverse effects from their mothers' alcohol use. A woman who drinks heavily has about a 40 % chance of bearing an affected child.

Noticeable symptoms: Facial malformations and retarded growth are usually evident at birth. Babies are often shorter and weigh less than normal. Developmental disability and behavioral problems make their appearance in early childhood.

Diagnosis: Congenital heart defects are usually diagnosed by means of an electrocardiogram.

Treatment options and outlook: Congenital heart defects can often be repaired surgically. Some behavioral problems can be improved with drugs. But retarded growth and developmental disability cannot be reversed.

Prevention: Doctors recommend that a woman refrain from drinking entirely if she is pregnant, is planning to become pregnant, suspects that she might be pregnant, or is nursing after childbirth.

Fetus
(FEE-tuhs)

BODY SYSTEM

For vertebrates that give birth to live young, the fetus is the developing animal between the embryo stage and birth. In humans an embryo that has attached itself to the uterine wall graduates to the fetal stage after five, eight, nine, or twelve weeks, depending on which expert you consult.

Size and location: The fetus grows in size from about 2 to 3 inches long to about 20 inches long. Just before birth the fully developed fetus ranges in size from a low of 5 pounds to as much as 15 pounds in extreme instances. The typical American baby weighs from 6 to 10 pounds at birth—half of all newborns weigh more than 7.5 pounds. Below a weight of 5 pounds, physicians identify the birth as *premature* (even if full term).

All of the growth before birth takes place within the uterus. The fetus and its mother's body cooperate to develop a special sac that is filled with *amniotic* (AAM-nee-OT-ihk) *fluid*, which cushions the fetus from bumps or other disturbances. The fetus is attached to its mother by the *umbilical* (um-BIHL-ih-kuhl) *cord*, which permits fluids, nutrients, and oxygen to pass from the mother to the fetus and the wastes from fetal growth and development to pass back to the mother. There is no direct exchange of blood, however. A

Just before birth

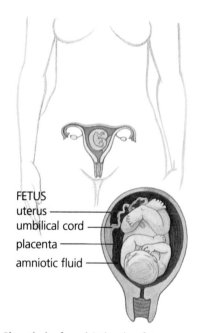

FETUS
uterus
umbilical cord
placenta
amniotic fluid

Shortly before birth, the fetus turns into a head-down position. It is readying itself to leave the safety of the amniotic sac and the nourishing placenta and to enter the world outside.

special organ called the *placenta* (pluh-SEHN-tuh) permits the exchange; a few blood cells sometimes do escape from mother to fetus or vice versa.

Role: The human fetus is well protected. During fetal development an individual produces functional organs and prepares for life in the open atmosphere and a new way of obtaining nourishment. At birth the umbilical cord is cut, and the lungs are put into action.

Conditions that affect the fetus: A few viruses, bacteria, and chemicals can pass through the placenta to interfere with fetal development. The best known of the viral agents that can interfere with development are rubella ("German" measles) and *cytomegalovirus*. A bacterium that can cross the placenta and infect the fetus is the one that causes syphilis. Chemicals that have induced errors in fetal development include thalidomide, one form of which interferes with the growth of fetal limbs. Chemicals that permit the fetus to grow but dramatically change the pattern of growth are called *teratogens* (tuh-RAAT-uh-juhnz). Some common medicines are teratogens when taken during certain stages of pregnancy, including isotretinoin (Accutane), phenytoin (Dilantin), and warfarin (Coumadin).

For many errors in fetal development the exact cause is not known. In some cases there may be genetic or chromosomal disorders, and in others the problem may be an unidentified virus.

When the fetus does not develop properly, one possible event is *spontaneous abortion* or *miscarriage*. The fetus is expelled from the body, and pregnancy is terminated. At later stages a fetus that has developed in a normal way may be born before the full growth term of 38 weeks. After about 25 weeks of development such a *premature baby* has a good chance of survival. Although there may be some physical problems that persist throughout life, especially with eye development, most premature infants are able to grow out of their early difficulties.

Poor maternal nutrition can also retard or alter development of the fetus. Sufficient folic acid is needed to prevent such development disorders as spina bifida and other neural tube defects.

INDEX

A

Abdominal wall defects **2**:99
Abruptio placentae **7**:5, **7**:10, **7**:14
Abscess **1**:9–10, **2**:16–17, **7**:35
Acetaminophen **6**:58
Achalasia **2**:56, **3**:102
Achilles tendon **8**:67–68
Achlorhydria **8**:22
Achondroplasia **4**:104, **7**:84–85
Acid reflux **4**:40
Acne **1**:10–12
Acoustic neuroma **3**:52, **8**:85
Acromegaly **4**:104, **6**:99
ACTH (adrenocorticotropic hormone) **4**:102
Actinomycetes **1**:97
Acupuncture **6**:59
Acute inflammatory polyneuropathy. *See* Guillain-Barré syndrome
Acute lymphocytic leukemia **5**:56
Acute nonlymphocytic leukemia **5**:56
Acute porphyrias **7**:3–4
Acute pyelonephritis **5**:36
Acyclovir **2**:88, **4**:36
ADA deficiency **1**:12–13, **5**:3
Addiction **3**:57, **3**:59–60
Addison, Thomas **4**:106
Addison's disease **1**:17, **1**:91, **4**:104, **4**:106, **8**:22
Adenine **4**:38
Adenoids **6**:26, **8**:62
Adenoma **8**:85
Adenomyosis **3**:90
Adenosine deaminase. *See* ADA deficiency
Adenoviruses **1**:87, **8**:103
ADH (antidiuretic hormone) **3**:29, **4**:103, **6**:98
Adrenal glands **1**:16–17, **3**:89, **6**:77–78
ADHD (attention-deficit/hyperactivity disorder) **1**:13–15
Adrenaline. *See* Epinephrine
Adult acne. *See* Rosacea
Aedes aegypti (mosquito) **3**:20
African sleeping sickness **6**:72
Afterbirth. *See* Placenta
Agent Orange **2**:66
Agoraphobia **6**:63

Agranulocytes **6**:92
Agranulocytosis **6**:24
AIDS (acquired immunodeficiency syndrome) **1**:17–22, **8**:13, **8**:15–16
and blood transfusions **1**:46
entry through birth canal **1**:109
history **1**:21
HIV testing **1**:19
and immune system **5**:4, **5**:5
as modern pandemic **3**:98
opportunistic diseases **6**:39–40
Pneumocystis carinii **1**:20, **6**:105–6
AIDS dementia **1**:20
Air sac **5**:66
Albinism **1**:22–24, **7**:104
Alcohol
and cancer **2**:35
fetal alcohol syndrome **1**:28, **3**:116–17
and frostbite **4**:19–20
nausea from **6**:14
Alcoholics Anonymous **1**:25, **1**:27, **5**:100
Alcoholism **1**:24–29
alcoholic siderosis **7**:88
and cirrhosis of the liver **2**:75
delirium tremens **1**:25, **3**:16–17
dementia **3**:19–20
Korsakoff's syndrome **1**:42
pancreatitis **6**:62–63
paranoia **6**:68
Alcohol poisoning **1**:24
ALD (adrenoleukodystrophy) **1**:29–30
Aldosterone **1**:16, **4**:102
Allele **4**:39
Allergens **1**:30–34, **1**:74, **4**:60
Allergic contact dermatitis **7**:32
Allergic purpura **7**:26
Allergic rhinitis. *See* Hay fever
Allergies **1**:30–34
from animals **6**:89
asthma **1**:73–77
hay fever **1**:31, **4**:60–62
and immune system **5**:3

and itching **5**:26
to stings **8**:20, **8**:21
Allodynia **7**:80
Alper, Tikva **7**:16
Alpha interferon **4**:90
ALS (amyotrophic lateral sclerosis) **1**:34–37, **6**:65
Altitude sickness. *See* Polycythemia
Alveoli **2**:109, **3**:82–83, **5**:66, **7**:39
Alzheimer's disease **1**:37–40
dementia **3**:19–20
Amblyopia **3**:106–7
Amebic dysentery **1**:9, **3**:60–62, **6**:72
Amenorrhea **1**:40–41
Amino acids **4**:39
Amnesia **1**:41–43, **2**:96
Amniocentesis **2**:70
Amniotic fluid **1**:117, **7**:12–13
Amphetamines **3**:58
Amyloidosis **8**:31–32
Amyotrophic lateral sclerosis. *See* ALS
Analgesia **7**:78
Anal itching **5**:26
Anaphylactic shock **1**:32, **7**:83, **8**:31
Anaphylaxis **5**:44
Anemia(s) **1**:43–47, **3**:114
aplastic **1**:44
pernicious **1**:44, **8**:22
in pregnancy **7**:9
thalassemia **1**:44, **8**:46–47
See also Sickle cell anemia
Anencephaly **6**:22
Anesthetics, local **6**:59
Aneurysm **1**:47–49, **2**:75, **5**:25, **8**:27
Angina **1**:50–51, **2**:40
Angiography **1**:79, **3**:75–76
Angioplasty **1**:80, **4**:79
Angiotensin **3**:33
Angle-closure glaucoma **4**:47
Animal bites **1**:54, **6**:91
snakebites **7**:112–14
spider bites **8**:1–2
Animal diseases and humans **1**:51–55
anthrax **1**:54, **1**:58–61
cryptosporidiosis **3**:4–5
Q fever **7**:27–28
rabies **1**:51, **1**:53, **6**:89, **7**:29–30

tularemia **8**:84
See also Pets and disease
Animal models **1**:54
Ankylosing spondylitis **1**:93, **1**:95
Anopheles mosquito **5**:80
Anorexia nervosa **1**:55–58
Anosmia **6**:26–27, **7**:78
Ant **8**:20
Antegrade amnesia **1**:41
Anterior compartment syndrome **4**:17
Anthracosis **3**:94
Anthrax **1**:54, **1**:58–61
bioterrorism **3**:81
Antibiotics
for gonorrhea **4**:49
for infants **5**:9
Antibodies **5**:2–3, **5**:75, **6**:92–93
in rheumatoid arthritis **7**:46
Anticoagulants **3**:76
Anticonvulsants **3**:100, **6**:58
Antidepressants **6**:58
Antidiuretic hormone. *See* ADH
Antigens **1**:32
Antihistamines **4**:61–62, **4**:99
Anti-inflammatory drugs **6**:58
Antipsychotic drugs **7**:68–69
Antiretrovirals **1**:19
Antivenin **7**:113
Anus **2**:98, **3**:47, **7**:35
Anuscope **4**:87
Anxiety **1**:61–63, **5**:99
Aorta **1**:70, **6**:79
coarctation of **2**:103
overriding of **2**:103
transposition of great vessels **2**:103–4
Aortic aneurysm **1**:47–49
Aortic stenosis **2**:102–3, **4**:69
Aortic valve **2**:102–3
Aphasia **1**:63–64
Aphthous ulcer **2**:38
Aplastic anemia **1**:44–45
Aplastic crisis **7**:87
Apnea **2**:62
See also Sleep apnea
Apocrine glands **3**:105
Apoplexy. *See* Stroke
Appendicitis **1**:64–66, **3**:48, **8**:23
Appendicular skeleton **7**:96–97

Melatonin **6**:95, **7**:59
Memory loss. *See* Amnesia
Ménière, Prosper **5**:92
Meniere's disease **1**:101, **3**:52, **5**:92–93
Meninges **5**:94, **8**:6
Meningitis **1**:99, **4**:84–85, **5**:94–96
Meningocele **1**:95, **8**:3–4
Menopause **6**:55
Menstrual pain **5**:96–98
Menstruation **8**:91
   cramps **2**:113–14
   PMS **6**:104–5
   toxic shock syndrome **8**:70–71
Mental illnesses **5**:98–101
   bipolar disorder **1**:106–8
   clinical depression **2**:79–83
   multiple personality syndrome **5**:115–16
   obsessive-compulsive disorder **6**:37–39
   panic attacks **6**:63–64
   paranoia **2**:81 **6**:67–69
   SAD (seasonal affective disorder) **7**:59–60
   schizophrenia **6**:68, **7**:67–69
Mental retardation. *See* Developmental disability
Menton, Greg **4**:115
Mercury poisoning **5**:104–6, **7**:9
Metastasis **2**:19, **2**:32, **5**:65, **7**:20, **7**:44
Metatarsus varus/adductus clubfoot **2**:84
Migraine **4**:63, **5**:101–4, **6**:14, **8**:24
Milia **7**:33
Miliaria **7**:33
Milk **5**:40–41
Minamata disease **5**:104–6
Minerals **3**:43–45
Miscarriage **3**:78, **3**:118
Mites **7**:63–64
Mitochondria **1**:5, **4**:38
Mitral stenosis and incompetence **5**:106–7, **7**:18
Mitral valve prolapse. *See* Prolapse of mitral valve
Mixed cerebral palsy **2**:50
Moles and freckles **5**:107–9
   and melanoma **5**:90–91
Molluscum contagiosum **7**:105
Molybdenum **3**:45

Mongolism. *See* Down syndrome
Monocytes **6**:92
Mononucleosis **2**:73, **5**:109–11
Monounsaturated fat **3**:42
Mood disorders **5**:99
Morning sickness **6**:14, **6**:16, **7**:7–8
Mosquito
   and dengue fever **3**:20, **3**:21
   and elephantiasis **3**:72–74, **8**:80
   and encephalitis **3**:85–86
   and malaria **5**:80–83, **6**:70, **6**:72, **8**:80
   and tropical diseases **8**:80, **8**:81
   and West Nile virus **8**:112
   and yellow fever **8**:118
Motion sickness **5**:111–13, **6**:14
   and balance **1**:101
   seasickness **6**:14, **7**:74–75
Motor neuron disease. *See* ALS
Mountain sickness **6**:118
MRI (magnetic resonance imaging) **3**:75
Mucocutaneous lymph node syndrome (MLNS). *See* Kawasaki disease
Mucous glands **3**:105
Mucus, in cystic fibrosis **3**:6–8
Multibacillary leprosy **5**:53
Multiple myeloma **5**:113–14
Multiple personality syndrome **5**:115–16
Multiple sclerosis **1**:91, **5**:116–18
Mumps **6**:1–3, **7**:61
Murine typhus **8**:87
Muscle(s) **6**:3–5
   cardiac **2**:40–41, **6**:3–4
   cramp **2**:113–14, **5**:50–51
   polymyositis **1**:88, **7**:1
   skeletal **6**:3–4, **7**:94–96
   smooth **6**:3–4, **7**:111
   strains **4**:17
   striated **6**:3
   tone **6**:4
Muscular dystrophy **1**:91, **6**:5–8
Mushrooms **4**:10
Mutation(s) **1**:12, **4**:34, **4**:40
Myasthenia gravis **1**:87, **1**:91, **6**:8–9
Mycoplasmal pneumonia **6**:107

Myelin sheath **5**:116, **6**:18, **8**:6
Myelomeningocele **1**:95, **8**:4–5
Myocardial infarction. *See* Heart attack
Myocarditis **2**:40, **6**:9–10
Myocardium **6**:9
Myopia **3**:107, **3**:109
   detached retina **3**:27
Myotonic dystrophy **6**:6
Myxedema **4**:105, **8**:52
Myxobacteria **1**:97

N

Nail infections and injuries **6**:11–13
   finger and toenail fungus **4**:7–8
   ingrown toenails **5**:16
Narcolepsy **6**:13–14
Narcotics **3**:59
Nasal polyps **6**:26, **7**:92
Natural killer cells **5**:75
Nausea **6**:14–16
   persistent **6**:16
   in pregnancy **7**:7–8
Nearsightedness **3**:107, **3**:109
Nebulizer **1**:76, **3**:3
Necrotizing fasciitis. *See* Flesh-eating bacteria
Neonatal acne **7**:33
Neonatal myasthenia **6**:8
Neonatal tetanus **8**:45
Nephritis. *See* Glomerulonephritis
Nephrogenic diabetes insipidus **3**:30
Nephrons **5**:38
Nephrotic syndrome **5**:36
Nerve blocks **6**:21, **6**:59
Nerve growth factor **4**:103
Nerves **6**:16–18
   damage **6**:65
   sciatic **7**:69
Nervous system **6**:18–20
Neuralgia **6**:20–21, **6**:23–24
Neural hearing loss **3**:12
Neurally mediated hypertension **2**:71, **2**:73
Neural plate **6**:21
Neural tube defects **1**:95, **1**:96, **6**:21–23
   spina bifida **6**:22, **8**:3–5
Neuritis. *See* Neuropathy
Neurofibrillary tangles **1**:38

Neurogenic dysphasia **3**:102
Neuroma, acoustic **3**:52
Neurons **6**:16
Neuropathy **6**:17–18, **6**:23–24
Neuroses **5**:98–99
Neutropenia **6**:24–25, **6**:93
Neurotransmitters **1**:61, **2**:86, **3**:59, **6**:17
Neutrophils **6**:24, **6**:92
Nevi. *See* Moles and freckles
Newborns. *See* Infants and disease
Niacin **6**:80–81, **8**:106, **8**:108
Nicotine **8**:58
Nicotine replacement therapy **8**:60
Night blindness **3**:110, **7**:42, **8**:105, **8**:108
Nighttime cramps. *See* Recumbency cramps
Nitrogen **1**:105–6
Nitroglycerin **2**:40
Nodular melanoma **5**:90–91
Non A, non B hepatitis **4**:94
Non-Hodgkin's lymphoma **5**:74, **5**:76–77
Nonsteroidal anti-inflammatory drugs (NSAIDs) **4**:64
Noradrenaline. *See* Norepinephrine
Norepinephrine **1**:16, **4**:103
Nose and throat conditions **6**:25–28
Nosebleed **6**:28–29
Nosocomial infections **6**:30–32
   health care **3**:79–80
   pneumonia **6**:107
   staph **8**:12
NSAIDs. *See* Nonsteroidal anti-inflammatory drugs
Nucleotides **4**:38
Numbness **6**:32–33, **7**:78
Nutrition. *See* Diet and disease
Nuts **3**:42
Nystagmus **3**:110

O

Obesity **6**:34–37
   diabetes mellitus type II ("adult-onset") **3**:35
Obsession **6**:38
Obsessive-compulsive disorder **6**:37–39

missing or supernumerary 3:23–24

periodontal disease **6:84–85, 8:**39

staining 3:22–23

toothache **8:62**

trauma 3:23

undersized 3:24

Temperature, body 4:1–3, 4:79–81, 4:118

Temporal arteritis 1:91, **8:39–40**

Temporomandibular disorder (TMD) 3:24, **8:56–57**
See also TMJ

Temporomandibular joint dysfunction. *See* TMJ

Tender points **4:**5

Tendinitis **8:**40–42, **8:**67

Tendon **8:**40, **8:67–68**

Tennis elbow and related problems 2:28, 5:60, **8:40–42**

Tenosynovitis **8:**41

Tension headache 4:63–64

Teratogens 3:118

Testes 3:89, 7:37, **8:42–43**

Testicular torsion **8:**43

Testosterone 4:103, **8:**42

Tetanus 1:99, 6:5, **8:44–45**

Tetracycline 1:11, 3:22

Tetralogy of Fallot 2:103

T4 cells 1:19, 1:20

Thalassemia 1:44, **8:46–47**

THC (chemical) 3:57

Thermometer 4:2–3

Thiamine. *See* Vitamin B₁

Threadworm (strongyloidiasis) **8:47–48**

Throat
nose and throat conditions **6:25–28**

sore **7:**116–17

strep **8:**24–25

tonsillitis 6:28, **8:60–62**

Thromboangiitis obliterans. *See* Buerger's disease

Thrombocytopenia 1:114

Thrombocytopenic purpura 3:67, 7:26

Thrombolytic drugs 3:76

Thrombophlebitis **8:48–50,** **8:**97, **8:**99

Thrush. *See* Candidiasis

Thymectomy **6:**9

Thymine 4:38

Thymomas **6:**8

Thymus 1:87, **8:50–51**
myasthenia gravis **6:8–9**

Thyroid gland 3:89, **8:51–52**
cartilage **5:**44

goiter **4:47–48**

Thyroid-stimulating hormone (TSH) 4:103, 6:98, **8:**52

Thyroxin (thyroxine) **4:**48, 4:103, **8:**51

TIA (transient ischemic attack) 5:25, 6:33, 8:27, **8:53–54**

Tic **8:54, 8:**79
Tourette's syndrome **8:68–69**

Tic douloureux **8:**54, **8:**79

Tick(s) 1:53, 3:71–72, **5:**70–73, 6:89, 7:51–53, **8:**80–81, **8:**84

Timolol **4:**46

Tinea capitis. *See* Ringworm.

Tinea cruris. *See* Jock itch

Tinea infections 4:21, 7:49

Tinea inguinalis. *See* Jock itch

Tinea pedis. *See* Athlete's foot

Tinea versicolor 4:21, 7:103–4

Tinnitus **8:**55

T lymphocytes. *See* T cells

TMD. *See* Temporomandibular disorder

TMJ (temporomandibular joint dysfunction) **8:55–57**

Tobacco and disease **8:57–60**
and cancer 2:35, **5:64–66**
See also Smoking

Toenails 4:7–8, 5:16, 6:11–13

Toe walking 2:50

Tongue 3:46

Tonic spasms 7:118

Tonometer 4:45–46

Tonsillitis **8:60–62**

Tonsils 5:73, 6:28, **8:**60

Toothache **8:**62

Tooth decay **8:63–66**

Tophi **4:**52

Topical anesthetics 4:44

Torn meniscus **8:66–67**

Torn or severed tendon **8:67–68**

Tourette, Gilles de la **8:**68

Tourette's syndrome **8:**54, **8:68–69**

Tourniquet 1:115

Toxemia. *See* Blood poisoning; Preeclampsia

Toxic enterocolitis 2:101

Toxic gastritis 4:27–28

Toxic shock syndrome **8:70–71**

Toxoplasmosis 6:72, **8:71–73**

Trachea 5:45, 6:26, 7:39, **8:73–74**

Tracheitis **8:**74

Tracheostomy **8:**74

Tracheotomy 3:49, **8:**74

Trachoma 1:100, **8:74–75**

Tranquilizers 3:58, 5:100–1

Transfusions. *See* Blood, transfusion

Transient ischemic attack. *See* TIA

Transplants
heart 4:77
and immune system **5:**4
liver 2:77, 2:99
rejection 1:90

Transposition of the great vessels 2:103–4

Transverse colon 5:42

Trauma, to teeth 3:23

Traveler's diarrhea. *See* Giardia

Trench mouth 3:22, **8:75–76**

Trichinosis 6:73, **8:76–77**

Trichomonas (trichomoniasis) 6:72, **8:16, 8:77–78**

Trichuriasis. *See* Whipworm

Tricuspid valve atresia 2:103

Trigeminal neuralgia 6:21, **8:**54, **8:**79

Trigger finger **8:**41

Triptans 5:103–4

Trisomy 3:54

Tropical diseases **8:**14, **8:80–81, 8:116–17**

Tropical sprue **8:**11

Tryptophan 6:80

TSH. *See* Thyroid-stimulating hormone

Tubal pregnancy 3:68, 3:112

Tubercules **8:**83

Tuberculosis 1:20, 1:52, 3:83, **8:82–83**
of bone 2:7
of spine 1:95

Tubules **8:**38

Tularemia **8:**84

Tumor, benign **8:85–86**

Tumor(s) 2:32
adrenal 1:16
and aphasia 1:64
benign **8:85–86**
esophageal 3:47
hearing loss from 3:12
kidney 5:37, **8:114–15**
salivary gland 3:47, 7:61
tongue 3:47
See also Cancer(s)

Tunnel vision **7:**42

Turner syndrome 2:70, 7:84

Twins 6:56

Twitch 6:4, 7:118
See also Tic

Typhoid fever 1:100, **8:86–87**

Typhus 1:100, **8:87–88**

Tyramine 5:103

U

Ulcerative colitis 1:91, 2:89–90, 2:117

Ulcers 1:100, 3:47, 8:22, 8:24, **8:89–90**

Ultrasound 1:49

Umbilical cord 3:117, 6:100, **7:**7, 7:38
compression or prolapse 2:61
stem cells **8:**17

Umbilical hernia 4:95–96

Undulant fevers 1:52

Ureter 3:103, 5:35

Urethra 3:103, 6:81, 7:37

Uric acid 4:51–53

Urinary bladder. *See* Bladder, infections

Urinary incontinence 5:6–7

Urine 1:112, 3:103–4, 5:38
protein in 7:6

Urticaria. *See* Hives

Urushiol 6:113–14

Uterus 1:109, 7:37, **8:91–92**
endometriosis 3:90–91
prolapse **8:**91–92

Utricle 1:101

Uvea **8:**92

Uveitis 1:91, **8:**92

V

Vaccination and disease **8:93–94**
anthrax 1:60, 1:61
BCG **8:**83
chicken pox 2:59
diphtheria 3:49
first against disease 1:61
hepatitis A 4:89
hepatitis B 4:91–92, 8:16
Hib 4:84–85, 5:95
HIV 1:19
influenza 3:95, 5:14
meningitis 5:95
mumps 6:3

Our thanks to the following organizations and persons who made the photographs used in this set possible:

Christ Episcopal Church Youth Program (Mary Millan)
Mount Vernon Teen Task Force (Chris Webb)
Putnam Family Support and Advocacy, Inc. (Pam Forde)

Photography assistant: Tania Gandy-Collins

MODELS
Roland Benson, Sally Bunch, Deirdre Burke, Kevin Chapin, Michael Clarke, Michelle Collins, Bryan Duggan, Germaine Elvy, Caitlin Faughnan, Imgard Kallenbach, Max Lipson, Lydia McCarthy, Amanda Moradel, Joshua Moradel, Veronica Moradel, Kate Peckham, Sara Pettinger, Mario Salinas, Heather Scogna, Halima Simmons, Wendy Sinclair, T.J. Trancynger, Rolando Walker, Deborah Whelan, Gregory Whelan, Francis Wick, Elaine Young, Leanne Young